My Experience with God!!

Something From Experience

by

Cathy Ann

ISBN: 1-4033-4168-0 (e-book)
ISBN: 1-4033-4169-9 (Paperback)
ISBN: 1-4033-7278-0 (Hardcover)

This book is printed on acid free paper.

1stBooks – rev. 10/16/02

A LITTLE BIT ABOUT ME!!

I've always had a wondering spirit. I love to travel and take photograph's. A firm belief in education, since there were some things in my life that haven't panned out over the years. I may have been in the closet or been backstage all these years and breaking out of this mode or shield that I have put around me, though it may not look like it, if we ever met. I always kept things to myself, but now that I am learning, I tell it like it is. There is always a time when someone else doesn't agree with you or may not believe that you have developed by learning from others, by watching.

I love animals, to taking walks in the woods, to creating something out of the ordinary. Some people might think that I'm a dreamer or won't make nothing of myself, but they have another thing coming. I will not stand for any more of this. It has to come out.

Cathy Ann

-INDEX-

INTRODUCTION

Experiences from all angels and all directions. I never notices it until recently. With going to the Crystal Cathedral, in Garden Grove, California. I guess every time I entered the church, from day one, I would get these powerful messages from Dr. Robert Schuller I or any of the other Ministers that were up there, plus from a few guest. Not only that, the feelings that I would get from God, Jesus or the Holy Spirit. In the time I have been there Jesus has shown me a lot of things, whether it was in a dream form or in reality. In a sense it brought some of the stories alive, so that I could put this book together. All this happened in the last ten years. The 1990's were the years of discover for me, in relationships, and where I should be in life. I needed the love and the respect from others. This doesn't mean I was looking for someone, but with a relationship with anyone at this point in time. This point in time is where I should being exploring some more in other areas and not listen to someone that I couldn't do something when I can, if I have the proper training.

You may think that some of the stories are so incredible that it couldn't be possible, but they are true. I am not trying to sell you a bag of onions, when you wanted a bag of potatoes. I could do the very same thing and tell you the same thing that I couldn't believe the story you told me. There are some stories that can't be explained. I say, sit there and think what God has done for you and your family lately. I bet you, you could come up with some whoppers. I just don't mean the hamburger, either.

Life is full of surprises. You never know what may come along, at whatever age. Whether, your sixteen or nine-two. You never know what God has up his sleeve for you. It could happen in the next ten minutes or in the time that it takes you to read this whole book or what you may get out of this. It could help you in some way that you have been dealing with for a long time or a very short period of time. There are some possibilities you know.

Wake-up, people. Life is not the same old thing, day after day, night after night. Go for those dreams, goals or ideas that you have in your head. God didn't put it there for nothing, you know!!

Wasn't September 11th, 2001 a day to remember and we moved to another level so we could be comfortable, whether we lost someone that day. For the ones that are unemployed, because you were working at the airport or in the travel industry or any other place that did have a massive lay off. What will you do? Just take another job somewhere or will your dream or goals come true? Which will it be?

I know, I'm making my move, are you?

CHAPTER ONE

TWISTER OF THE MIND!!!

What's this world coming too? There are so many things that are going on that could be a mind twister, wouldn't you think? That will blow you away. With all the killings, rapes, drive by shootings, to finding yourself somewhere in the world of the Lord, to dealing with something that you would never expected in your life time, even though there was a family history of this disease in your family. Always thinking that you would beat the odds, but didn't and to top it off, trying to find a church that was meant for you to be in.

I (Cathy) was in that kind of situation. For so many years I was unhappy, not satisfied with the church I was going to. I always thought as long as you believed in the Lord, that things would be all right. I had been doing this for so many years, but just getting by. Sure, I would get some of my prayers answered, but it took so long to get some of them. Since nineteen ninety, things were changing. My feelings were going all over the place.

I first noticed it in July of that year, when I got the flight information I asked for, from my aunt. Before I ever read the information or the little note that she put onto the back of it, starting to get some tickets to the "PRICE IS RIGHT". When I lifted the envelope I had this surge of energy from it. It was telling me something more than the information that was on the envelope and the sheet of paper. That something was going to happen and that it would be big time. I just hoped that it wouldn't be my aunt and that she couldn't come with her friend. I started to praying. I prayed so hard, till I was blue in the face. I didn't know what God or the Devil were planning for one of my family members. I didn't know that it would be cousin Edith. I was just hoping that it wasn't my aunt Debbie, because it took me twenty years to this point. Maybe even longer, in letters or in person. That there were so many things out here that it wasn't even funny. I prayed. I asked the Lord Jesus to please not let it be her and to show her a sign that it would be all right for her to leave that situation. From that point on, I was totally in the dark. I had nothing to fall back on. There was no word of any kind, no nothing. I was on pins and needles from that time forward, until her arrival on August 29, 1990. Six weeks of not knowing what was going on. That was some torment. I found out what was eating at me for those six weeks. A week before Debbie was suppose to come to Los Angeles. My youngest cousin Edith was in a very serious car accident. If only that truck had passed there only ten minutes earlier or ten minutes later, then none of this would of happened. She even died twice, but Jesus had used her as his angel of good news and for whatever other reason or reasons, he put into her mind. Jesus had Edith tell her mother that she still was going to California and that everything will be all right. If it was someone else, that told her that, I don't think that she would of come. Or if things turned out a little differently. That will be the sixty-four thousand dollar question for this story. I was at ease when I got the answers to my questions when Debbie told us the story about Edith.

On the last day that Debbie and Kim were here in California. I took them to the Crystal Cathedral on Tuesday before they left. It was the topping for their cakes that they made for themselves. It was all thrills and the benefits that went on their cakes. I guess Jesus had other plans for me and was telling me or asking me to come to the Crystal Cathedral. It didn't even dawn on me, that this church would do the trick for me. It wasn't until five years later, when I did join the church.

Though it had to take something so shocking and so scary to get on the ball here. It isn't easy dealing with cancer at all. It's something that I wouldn't want to deal with again. It was like Jesus was taking by the sent of my pants and lifted me up and just shaking me. Just to tell me to wake up to the fact that I should be at the Crystal Cathedral. Like a father tell his child to straighten out or listen up.

I first notice it when I started going over to U.C.I. Medical Center, in the city of Orange. As I passed the church I started hearing things, like, this is your new church home, to you'll be happy here. In time things will come to you. That everything doesn't come all at once. It may seem like it at the time, with everyone wanting to see you, to work related things that had to be handled.

But Jesus knew that I had to much to handle at this present time. I was scared out of my wits and didn't want to die. He knew that I was a fighter and that I wanted to do something. To make my mark in life. There was this certain void in there. That there was something I had to do and to have a lot better life then I was having at this present time. That I shouldn't be taking any things, just because I needed a job. Why should I allow myself to only take jobs that only pay five dollars an hour, when other people were getting eight to ten dollars an hour, maybe even more. That they don't even speak English no less. I am not against people that are from other countries and taking our jobs, but when and what is my purpose in life? Why couldn't I land a job that pays well and that I liked very much and start from there. I guess Jesus doesn't think that's the ideal and wants me to go through a lesson or two and that anything is better than nothing. In a way, I agree with that, but I've been doing this for so long, that it hurts. What am I suppose to do, wait till I'm a little old lady from Pasadena, before something will happen.

3

For three weeks going on four, I was going back and forth to the Medical Center. I took all the tests that they wanted me to have. You name it, I had it. I was getting to the point of a nervous break down, because I wondered when this was going to end. I didn't want to have a hysterectomy, but when Dr. White called me in, to talk to me. That it wasn't going to be that exploratory surgery, and we have to go the whole nine yards and take everything. I just had to let it all out.

"That it wasn't fair, that I couldn't have at least one child. With all these woman that have baby after baby, then they have the child and leave it on a door step somewhere. How could a person do that? Or that the mother or father would molest the child in some way to killing the child or just throw them into a bid dump stir and just walking away, while it was still crying. It's a crying shame on their part.

Dr. White suggested adopting a child. Great idea, but I don't think so. It's not the same. I wanted to go through the whole nine yards, from beginning to end. All the doctors that I saw, thought I was the greatest patient they ever had. I don't think that they will ever have another patient like me. Somehow humor kicked in there somewhere, even right to the end. Right before I went into the operating room. David, (a male nurse) came into the room where I was and told me what I needed to know and asked if I had any questions. I responded by saying, "Yes, how long is the operation? He answered by saying, "Oh, on a normal hysterectomy about two, two and a half hours and asked why? I responded by saying, "Oh, because I have an appointment at six o'clock with Kevin Costner, about this movie deal that we have going on or that will happened once everything is settled." Everyone smiled and thought that it was a cute joke. They didn't know whether I was joking or not. It could have been true for all they knew. The laugh could be on them, but of course at the time, it wasn't true, but who knows someday.

Maybe he'll do one of my stories, or just meet him at some gathering of Hollywood's most greatest. I am not just dreaming about it.

I didn't know that day. I would be in the operating room for four hours, if that nurse told me that it was only a two or two and a half hours operation. They must of had an hour and a half for lunch maybe, who knows. It may have been a lot worse than they thought. To top that off, they had put me into Intensive Care. When I get sick, I get sick.

During the middle of the night, I woke up, while in the Intensive Care and I must have been coming out of it more and with them taking all the necessary vital signs every few minutes as they do in that unit. I felt like I was still dopey. I didn't even open my eyes and I turned my head and asked the nurse, "I wish you nice people would leave me alone. I would like to get a good night sleep. I'm tired." Sue (the nurse) knew that I must of been still out of it and that I didn't know where I was at. With her sweet and gentle way, she said this, "You'll be getting plenty of sleep tomorrow and that you're in Intensive Care Unit." It satisfied me for the moment. I turned my head and went back to sleep. To me, Sue was an angel. What she said was a comforting to know.

An hour or two later, when I opened my eyes wide. I found myself on a elevator. I was surprised and confused. I asked if we were headed back to the operating room, once again. I may have thought it was the first time or that something might of happened and they needed to go back in there or that the incision had reopened. A lot of things were going through my mind, until I got the answer or answers from Peter, (one of the male nurses.) He must of realized that I didn't know that I was in the intensive care unit and was just coming out of it.

I was happy with the answers that Peter gave me and went for the ride to see where they were going to take me. A ride of a life time, too. We were going around corners and going this way and that way, until we ended up in this one room with one bed in it. Tammy (a nurse) didn't like the bed that was there and asked if we could play musical beds. Once that was done. Peter had the nerve to ask me if I could move from the bed I was in to the one they just brought. I guess they didn't want to do that trick they always do with the sheets, because of my weight.

I responded by saying that, "I would give it an old school try, but if I can't, you have to help me. It's not going to be easy!" I said.

This was not an easy thing for me to do. Every time I moved, it hurt like hell. It was something else to go through. Cancer is nothing to fool around with. Moving so slowly like a snail crossing a sidewalk without being escargot. It must of taken me at least five minutes. I was afraid of reopening the incision. The pain was so great. I knew that I never wanted to go through another operation again. Those knives must have been razor shape. I thought I was finished, but Peter asked me to do it one more time. I was to close to the edge to suit him. Then everyone was satisfied.

To me, it was a job and a half. I knew I needed to take a nap after doing all that. I asked Tammy for a pain killer. A few minutes later, she brought me one. It's not easy being down and out. No matter how major or minors it is. I felt useless, like a bag of potatoes sitting in a store bin somewhere. Afraid to move, with tubes coming out of you left and right. The incision was a seven or seven and a half inches long and holding it together were all these staples. Now I know how a box or two or more pieces of paper feel when they are stapled together.

Whatever the stuff they had used to knock me out, did a number on me. Not only that they must have given me another shot of that stuff. Whatever it's name was, if it could knock me out, it could knock out an elephant. I am very serious when I say that. I'm the type that doesn't like to be lying around. I may not look the type that would be active, but I like to be in the middle of things. I am the type of person, but it seems no one believes me, from helping someone, (in anything) to being a part of something. I don't like being alone. I'm the type that likes to be with people, but I am afraid that some people do not understand me sometimes. Just because I am more down to earth and say things in a very simple way. Doesn't mean that I am some kind of alien from another planet. Give me a break, please.

I thought that the operation was bad enough, but it wasn't. The chemotherapy had beat it by a long run. Sick as sick can be. It might of saved my life by a long shot, but the experience to me was no picnic and no laughing matter. Reporting the Cancer Center at eight o'clock in the morning and not getting out of there until five-thirty or six that night. Nine hours of this ordeal was something else. With two bottle and a bag of the Chemo. I was beginning to think that the bottle was always going to be there. I knew that I wasn't going to turn to any other bottles of any kind. It got so tiring after awhile. One week being sick, that I couldn't do anything. Afraid of doing anything for at least a week, or until I felt assured enough to be out in the world again. I thought I would never finish those six treatments. It felt like every time I turned around, it was time to go to the Cancer Center at the U.C.I. Medical Center, in the city of Orange. I was glad that all the doctors were so happy that things were working out the way that it did. I wanted this part to end very soon. Finally, graduation day. I was so happy, that it was out of this world. It was a Christmas present from Dr. Black and his staff. With the six treatment did the trick and I wouldn't have to go back for any more.

For those six months and six treatments. I thought I was doing jail sentence of some kind, for doing what I did to my body. Cancer is the one that gets the sentence and I never want to see it ever again.

After being released from the Doctor's care. It was hard getting back into the working world once again. I tired the Temporary Services, but all I kept hearing was, we haven't anything. How could they stay in business if they don't have anything. Would someone answer me that question? Or they only paid five dollars an hour and never give their employees an incentive. Or only sent them to the same place all the time. That's no fun. The minimum wage should be at least seven dollars an hour by now. (In 1995.) I like to see some of the rich people live on just five dollars an hour, then they know what the hell I am talking about.

It was hard getting back into the work force, because of the Cancer. Some people may of thought that Cancer was contagious and the fact they would get it and didn't want to go through what I did. They may even of thought they would even look terrible and lose a lot of weight or even die. With all the different cultures here in Southern California. There different beliefs and customs. A person could be shut out of the work force so fast, because of an illness. An illness that only effects the patient and not anyone else. What is it with some people. They better start learning about some things. That's all I've got to say on that subject.

This is when I decided to move into a different career. A career that is not an easy occupation to get into. Publishing is something not to fool with. Unless by chance you have been around it all your life or know someone in the business and that doesn't guarantee anything, unless it is meant for you to be a published author with some article at first or go directly to writing that novel you always kept talking about and it gets published and it's a best seller and then Hollywood or from somewhere else, makes you an offer to make your story into a movie. It's all in the cards.

Sometimes it's not what you know, it's who you know. I wish when I send whatever story somewhere and they are fascinated with my story I sent to them.

I am just taking what I can to survive and I'll kept on trying until I am that little old lady from Pasadena. Life is funny sometimes. You never know what may come across you path. Take whatever opportunities it may be. It may not come your way ever again. It doesn't knock twice. I wish I had an opportunity, from somewhere, anywhere.

Cancer is nothing to fool around with. Sure it is a shocker to find out this information that you have Cancer in your body somewhere, but when you come out of it. Please don't take the road that is so dark and think bad thoughts. Think on the bright side. Your family and friends. Think of them. Life would be a lot different without you. Think of the story called, "It's A Wonderful Life" with James Stewart. Then and only then you will understand. Life might be hard, but without you and you alone, the chain will be broken. Someone will need you for that last minute kiss on the forehead. Maybe just to get your support (just to be in their corner.)

So you are important, you know.

Chapter Two

The Chosen

What does it take to be one of the chosen ones? It is not only the ones that are true believers, or the ones that go to church every Sunday, and only do good things, and they read the Bible, so many times a day. To thinking to themselves that they are saints. That they are so pure and so high and mighty. No, it's not about the ones that go to church every Sunday and read the Bible so many times a day or the ones that think that they are so high and mighty and know every verse in the Bible by heart. That maybe great to know, but that isn't the only thing that God is looking for. What happens to the lost little lambs, or the ones that needs His help in so many ways. To people that don't even believe in Him. To a person that believes in Him, but always gets on the wrong road somehow or they think it is the right one, but finds out, that it isn't the right one, after all. To someone that has grown up with Him, but was confused and a Puzzled Child To A Puzzled Woman. We all were put onto the earth, for a reason. Not just for some, but for everyone. The reasons and the lessons are different, but we all end up at the same gates of Heaven and will be judged by God.

What if you were one of the chosen ones and didn't even know it? What would you say to that? Would you be shocked or surprised or even in the state of non-believers? What would be your answer be? Yes, you always know that you were special and that you have all these talents from point A to Z, but those may of gotten you where you're at today, but somewhere down the road, you are driven to be at a certain place on a certain day, whether you are a member of that church or not. That day may still come and on this day the Holy Spirit will bless you, in some way. To show you a light that you may of never seen before.

Lets say that you were this person. Lets say my name is Dee Dee. For some strange reason, you knew that you were special. (yes, we're all special, but this is a step further then normal.) Acting like any other child. Not really thinking anything was out of the norm. At the age of seven or eight. I gone to my grandfathers attic as I always did in the past, but this time, I was alone and I was looking around for whatever I maybe looking for. I could feel that I wasn't alone. The force or the being or whatever I had felt was a strong one. I looked around the room, but didn't see anything or anyone. At this time, I didn't understand it and had left that floor, but afterwards, I knew I was special.

Despite whether happened to me from that day in nineteen fifty-eight to the year nineteen seventy was a roller coaster of roller coaster!! The ups and downs that I gone through. Basically by myself, but I didn't choose to be. I wanted more out of life, but didn't get it, because I didn't know how to get it. With only my other to rely on. A mother that was over protective and didn't want me to be doing certain things. Even the normal things that a person does at that age. I, some times felt like an outcast. With no real education and a figure that was out of this world. (Of being two hundred and fifty pounds.) (To people that just went on doing what they did of name calling and all the wise cracks from the bullies.) It doesn't bother me, now. I rather be on the heavy side then be at the opposite end of the stick and be too thin. That's no good either. Though I would like to lose that hundred and twenty pounds is what I would like to do, but I am not busy enough. At this time, it wasn't time for me to be thinking of losing the weight. It was time for me to be honored and to be blessed by God. It was some day, but I didn't think that it would be. I treated it like any ordinary day.

This was like any other day. I gone to work and treated it like any other day. Of course, when you not expecting something, that's when something usually happens. Life is full of surprises. This was one of my surprises.

After spending a few hours with some friends at the V.F.W. Hall in Hasbrook Heights. Pat dropped me off, along with my grandmother, since we lived right across the street from each other. I was so glad to walk into my studio apartment, that I had. So that I could have some time for myself, but before I could do anything, I had to take out little Tina, for her nightly walk. (Tina was my little dog.)

Since it was after eleven o'clock at night. Even in the nineteen seventies, a person had to watch out for themselves. I closed the door to my studio apartment, then open the door to the outside world, which could be a jungle out there. We walked across the porch and down the stairs. We walked about twenty feet across the lawn to the first of many stops. As Tina was doing her thing. I looked around. A person never knows what may happen. But this night, was a special night. Who knew it was going to be this way. Then, I looked into the sky. The stars were shining brightly. There were a few clouds here and there, but nothing to worry about. Tina pulled me a few steps down the side walk to another location. I repeated the same scenario. I wasn't going to take any chances. For the second time, I found myself looking into the sky. Everything was the same. The only difference was the location. It didn't dawn on me what was going to happen. Again, we moved another few feet going westbound on Atlantic St. Again I looked around, and for the third time, I looked into the sky. Still everything was the same.

Then I knew something was out of the norm here. I said, "What gives, Lord? What is the meaning of this?

Then things started to happen in the sky. This one average dark gray could came from one direction and another one came from the other direction. They acted like curtains. Joining together at this one point. A moment later, there was this bright light. The clouds reopened to start the show at hand. I had no idea of what the hey was going on here. I just stood there like this was a normal thing to do. What I saw was this bright light. It was shape like the moon, but this wasn't the moon. It was too bright and it had a face. This was overwhelming for me. My feelings were mixed, but mostly honored. The bright light had started to moving closer and closer to me. Then all of a sudden it had stopped, to almost to where I could touch it, but of course, I couldn't. The Holy Spirit started to talk with me, but there was no volume. I couldn't hear a thing. It didn't make any sense to me. Of why God or the Holy Spirit would go through all that trouble to do something like that, I couldn't understand it, at the time.

After God or the Holy Spirit said, whatever He was going to say to me. He gone back to the first place He was seen in the sky. Those very same clouds that brought Him here, had come and gone in front of Him again, just like before. God just disappeared. Then, the clouds went there separated once again.

At this point, I got chilled and told Tina to come and that we should go into the apartment and get a good night sleep. I guess I was to stunned or in shock of some kind. I didn't know what to make of this surprise that I got from God.

By morning, I acted like nothing happened and acted like I do every morning and did what I generally do and went to work. From that morning on, to this day. I gone to a couple of people, but they didn't have the right answers I was looking for. I had to find the answer to it. I mentioned it to Dr. Beverly Muffin one day and she explained it to me. In short, because Dr. Muffin can really explain away some times. That I was one of the chosen ones and that He was telling me some things that would becoming in your near future. Some references and how I should handle the situation and not to panic over it. That one day, I would be seeing something so unbelievable. Then when I mentioned it to Ken Leestma. He said, that it wasn't God and a few other things.

Well, that got me more confused. I thought that I was back at square one once again. It was time to get to the bottom of this, because I knew that it had some meaning and some importance. Though it didn't bother me or effect me in anyway for twenty-six years. Till it surfaced in nineteen ninety-six, when I first mentioned it to Beverly. Maybe, this is where things are going to start happening, I have no idea.

I do have this feeling that something is going to happen big time, that I and the other people that have been touched by God, that we will meet someday at the church and will be touched by the Holy Spirit.

My thoughts are that at this time, that the Holy Spirit is setting something up, and is starting something in motion. A chain of events have to happen first, then the Holy Spirit will come or whatever things do happens in whoever life will happen. Have patients, as I must wait also.

Keep with your prayer and they will be answered in due time, it may not be the time that you chose, but its Gods choosing to do it in His time. He knows what is best for us.

Chapter Three

FIRE IN THE SOUL

What is the soul? Are our souls the ones that guide us to what we are going to be in life, whether it comes early or later in our lives, because we went on a different road or pathway, for a number of reasons. Is it something that is suppose to happen at the age that it does happen. Then, how come with some people it comes sooner, then others? Is it because they are suppose to learn some lessons, along the way, or pay the price. It maybe, because, we are suppose to do something else first, but if that's the case. How could someone find out what the answer is? Sure, there is prayer, but lets say you pray until you blue in the face, about this problem, or concern, and you know that God Jesus, has heard it, despite if you used the same words or not. It may have been changed to give it a little flavoring, to see if that worked, but it didn't work. Or you think the answer is taking too long, from Jesus, because you would like the answer right away. It maybe because you had this idea in your brain for this long period of time, but thought that it would never happen, because it would be a million to one odds that you would get it. This is where people are mistaken or they only try a couple of times and just give up. Do not give up the ship!! Then sometime down the road Jack and Jill's ship does come in, and they are not doing it any more. Maybe it was playing cards, or a day at the track, (whether it is the horse or any other track.) It could be that you were playing bingo, and you were so close and always needed that one number to get that prize, (whether it was for a bag of potatoes or apples, to something like two hundred dollars.) Maybe your game is Keno, and you get your four numbers and gotten a number of them, but that wasn't satisfying, because you may want the money to get yourself

15

a new car, of some kind. You may of wanted to do something nice for Auntie Em or your cousin Thomas, because he has not been doing so good and you figure that he needs more opportunities in his life, then what his father or grandmother could ever do for him. Something he would never have done, if it never came his way.

Despite what the money was used for, maybe you weren't meant to win it, at the time that you chose to win it. It always has to come from God. He may think that you would have to pay the price, by earning it, yourself. I know that sounds cruel, but life is not a bed of roses and why should you have everything that you wanted out of life, right then and there. What is this, people? Yes, everyone has been in that same boat, unless you came from a rich family and you get your way all the time, because you maybe the favorite. There is usually one in a family, whether or not we are rich or poor.

I am just like everyone else. I (Cathy) would like to know how it feels to be rich and powerful. It doesn't mean that I would be famous in whatever, but I just don't want to be rich for a day, or a month, but for the rest of my days and do those nice things for whoever. I am not dreaming this. I will do it, if it does come my way.

I don't know about anyone else, but with me, I get recurring dreams. They have been only two in my life that I remember, and the second is driving me nuts. I believe that was the only thing I dream about all night, and even in my daydreams, it would happen. It was the only thing I could think about. I had wondered if this was a message from God, Jesus or the Holy Spirit. I had started to pay. Is this suppose to happen in my near future, or maybe a year or two down the road or what? I had no idea. This is a new journey for me. I do not know where this is leading me. Sure, there is the Lottery, but there was another concern that I had. It was to get some of my stories into print. Since, none of the magazines, not the publishers were taking my short stories or my books. I wondered when I was going to start on my journey with this. There were no answers from the people that do have a copy. They may have put them into the church paper, and wouldn't know the answer one way or another until that month edition came out. Though they say, "No news, is good news, when you don't hear anything, but at least for me, I wish that they would at least drop a note of some kind. Or just send back the article or story in question. I know things don't always come right away, but I've been fishing for the longest time. In the end, there have been no bites. If there were, it was usually they would want you to put in a certain percentage of the money and then take it from there. That's not the road that I want to take, even if I did have the money, because I'm not going to do all the work and then invest besides. Plus go the long way around to get this books onto the market.

Despite, what your dream or your ideas or goals are, keep on moving down the road with them. Something could happen at anytime and any place. You never know who you might meet with the next few minutes, to the next day. Keep on talking about it. Talk with anyone that you may know, whether it's in your church, work, or a place of recreation. You have to start somewhere. Even if it's the bottom of the Totem Pole, but at least it's a start. You may not like it, but if that's the case. There is nothing we could do about it, is there?

I'm willing to try. Why not you? My head is barely above the water, but I'm still hoping that one day, something will come my way. Whether it's the lottery or anything I touch that deals with money, so I could do the great things that I was told in my dream. Just believe in hope faith and in Jesus Christ.

Chapter Four
Something Too Remember

What is this? What is this world coming to? Is it all work and no play? Do we have to work ourselves to death to make ends meet? The answer of course is, no! Then why do we become work alcoholics, with by working seven days a week at the same place, the same hours, and working at a place that doesn't make us happy and the pay is very lousy? Why not do what your heart tells you? Go after it, I dare you! Life is to short for this hogwash. If you want to be a painter, then be a painter, if you want to be a pilot, then go for that, but just don't sit there like a bump on a log. Be happy! Get those plans into operation!! Please don't waste your time on this. Go on. Even if it's to write an article or that novel you kept talking about. No matter the age, go for it! Is there something that you always wanted to do, but never took the time to do it. When do we take a break from this madness? Maybe that's why there are so many people are dying so young from heartaches and other things. It is that weekend in the mountains or the shore, to the grand trip to Europe somewhere, wherever your little heart desires, be happy for a change. Why always be there when someone else may need you? Take the time for yourself and feel a lot better. Then when you do come back and you will fee vibrant. Others will appreciate you more and you could do a lot more and in the end, they will show their appreciation to you.

(IN A RAISE I HOPE!!!!)

At this time in my life. I (Cathy) had to take a break from this rat race I was living. Enough is enough. I love the work, but I was getting to the point of being on the verge of a nervous break down. I couldn't take it anymore. I worked for three years straight with no breaks whatsoever. To tell you the truth, I do not know where I got the energy and the strength from, but pulled through with flying colors. There were days I worked, twelve, fourteen, to sixteen hours a day, depending on the stage of the game.

I met this man, by the name of John. He was very attractive looking man. His height was five-eight with light brown hair and blue eyes. His weight was about two hundred and twenty five pounds. He worked in the entertainment business. The first time I saw him was in a soap-opera. That lasted for six years. I had a crush on him. His true name will not be mentioned.

We worked on this project together. At first it was the book and second the script and then getting a studio to do the movie and last but not least to make the movie. Through each stage, the ideas were coming like crazy. It was some kind of miracles of sorts. If I didn't have anything, then John would come up with something. The chemistry was there from day one. The aura was so bright, that a person would need to wear a pair of sunglasses when they came near us. It was something special. It was meant for us to have this project together. We both didn't why, but it had just happened. Neither one of us couldn't explain it to ourselves or to anyone else. It was just magic. There are no words to explain the relationship between us.

The scene opens up on the last day of shooting the movie. At this time it was all in the can, (everything was done.) We were having a farewell party for this job well-done. The spread they had laid out was out of this world. There were all kinds of foods. You could eat to your hearts content, if you wanted too. There were all kinds of drinks. A person would go hungry or thirsty.

After grabbing a plate of food. I walked around to find a spot to sit down. When I had gotten by the plants. I heard this two woman talking. I stopped for a moment. They didn't see me. I heard my name mentioned. Tracy (the first woman, that was talking) had thought that there was something between John and myself and telling June her interruption of her point of view. I had to almost laugh at this. Of what people will do in their spare time. June was agreeing with Tracy. Of course I didn't want it to go any further than that. I put my two cents in it. My performance was Oscar bound. I should become an actress, but I don't think so, because I am not going into that field.

"Pardon me, ladies, but don't you have anything better to do then to talk about something that isn't true. Just because you see two people together all the time doesn't mean that there is something going on between them. Tracy, how could you start something like this, or have you and June been talking all the time while the movie was being made? What did you talk about? Do they really go together? Did you think that we had sex and wondered how we did it, since we are on the heavy side. Did you go through all the stages of conversation? What is it with you two? There is no truth in what you're saying. I just wish that you would cut it out". I said. "Well I heard that it was true, that you and John were going out! I've noticed a difference in John and how he had been behaving on this project and when he is with you that his face lights up and seemed that he was in love. You had that same kind of look. What do you expect people to think? I could see from day one that there was something there. You know you can not fool people you know and with that wedding band that you keep wearing. What do you expect?" said June.

"I expect nothing, if you think that? John and I are not having an affair and we both have other spouses. You are awful mistaken. I do not have an affair with someone that has a wife, girlfriend, or is living with someone. I suggest that you pick on someone else. You have the wrong person to fool with". I said.

"Oh is that so? Then why did you spend so much time at John's home, if you weren't having an affair? Answer me that, will you?" said Tracy.

"Very simple, my good woman, it was all work related. Plus the fact of getting the hell out of here at a unreasonable hour of the night. John's home was a lot closer than mine. I don't think that there way anything wrong with that. He didn't want me to get an apartment or to spend the extra money for another place. Which I didn't mind doing. You better think again. This is how people get into trouble with others." I said. "Are you trying to threaten me?" said Tracy. "No, I am just warning you to butt out of my business. There is no affair of any kind. I am not the one that you want to talk about!" I said.

"That's what you think! I'll talk about anyone I feel like. This is a free country. I have free speech. I have the first amendment to rely on." said Tracy. "Yes, she does have the first amendment and if this goes any further than that I would be on Tracy's side. There is two against one, so there" said June. (With a face could kill if anyone had looked at it. She was ugly as sin. Whoever went for her has to be a little bit off his rocker or be desperate to have some sex. Her weight was about a hundred and forty and she stood at five-three. A woman I wouldn't go for, if I was gay. Her personality stunk in the worst way.)

"Oh don't give me this shit. I don't need that like a whole in the head. You two are the ones that started this whole thing. If you didn't need to gossip about something. You are spreading lies that's what I am talking about. I can get you both for perjury, if it ever go that far. So don't give me all this garbage, because that's all it is to me. Because one of these days you will get into very serious trouble with the direction that you are going. All you are, is a pair of tramps in my book and you're nothing but trouble. So just stay the hell away from me." I said. (I gave them a look that kill if it had too.)

Unknown to the three of us, John was standing on the other side of the plant. There were two separate entry's to the room. I was glad that he had heard everything that was said, especially what those tramps said. Also across the room, June and Tracy's husbands were watching the whole thing. Tom and Walter walked across the room to see what the hell was going on. They (the husbands) knew what was going on, in a sense, but wanted to stop it before it got any further. Before it go to ugly and before someone else had notices what was going on here. John came around the plants, when he had seen Tom and Walter coming over to the fighting ring. So there wouldn't be a real show of shows. John wanted this right to go smoothly as possible. If Tracy and June kept on with their actions. John would have to tell them to leave. He wasn't going to put up with that kind of nonsense either and he wouldn't have them on his film crew ever again. He doesn't like people that are liars or trouble makers. If they called him to see if there was something going on, (work wise) all he would tell them that he has nothing or that he has all the people that he needs. They were both finished in his book. Two woman that were jealous and wanted some of that special treatment that I was getting from John. I do not know where those two were coming from, when everyone was married to someone else, expect little ole me. I think that June and Tracy wanted to get a piece of the action, is all what they wanted. Which there was none. It was all work, there was no playing whatsoever. It was three years of hard work, nonstop. If it was one thing, it was something else. I was so glad that John had said that's a rap and put it into the can. It is all over; done with. Let's party! Bring on the refreshments!

By this time, I was ready to get on with it. It was ready to fight with one of them or the both of them. Insult after

insult was quite enough. Everyone was red as a tomato.
Tracy got the worse of it though, just before they had left
the room, I had thrown the plate of food all over her. She
was a mess. With a little bit of red tomato sauce, the grease
from the sausage and to top it off, some of the salad with
French dressing. When I do a whopper, I do a whopper. I
don't do it just half way, I go the whole nine yards. There is
no fooling around at this fight. Tracy will remember this
night for the rest of her life. June was in some kind of
shock. She didn't know what to make of this now. Walter
and June helped Tracy to her dressing room, so she could
get cleaned up. While Tom was talking to John, the words
weren't pleasant. John had to tell Tom that both of them
were fired. And the fact he never wanted to see them ever
again. He didn't like the way they operate. If he known this
three years ago, he wouldn't of hired them in the first place.
John agreed with me, that they were both tramps and he
didn't like them at all, especially after tonight. At this point
everyone was watching what was going on and were talking
with each other and wondered what this was all about!

John turned to the group and told them, "Listen ladies
and gentlemen, everything is all right. There is nothing to be
concerned about. Everything is fine. Lets go on with the
activities here at hand.

Tom didn't like what John said, but didn't say anything,
because he didn't want to make another scene. Once was
enough for the night. He turned and left. So disgusted with
what had happened with the girls and to top it off, what
John had just said. Tom just wanted to go home and forget
about the whole matter. He figured that tomorrow will be a
better day and that John will have forgotten all about his in
time. I just hoped that he didn't hold his breath, because
John did not forget so soon or did he a few months down
the road. Some people do not give up so easily. A job is a
job, but when a person makes a mistake then they should go

on and find some other job. That's life for you. Some people do not forgive when it's something that is not right to do.

An hour later, I told John that was going home. I had enough for one night and that I would talk with him in a couple of days. At this point in time I needed a well deserved rest. Three months would do the trick. I know exactly where to go, to where no one would fine me. The job was great, but I also needed the time to get away for awhile. I needed my own space. John knew this from the start, but he had forgotten and I had to explain it to him all over again. Besides, I wanted some of this heat to blow over. I like John very much, but with him married to Sharon, there was nothing that we could do. I wasn't going to let it get out of hand or go any further than it already did. Sharon and John were a nice couple and I wasn't about to break them up. It will be a cold day in hell before that happens. I'm sure John was thinking the same thing. It was all on a profession level, though sometimes I don't know about that man, because of the was that he was acting.

Twenty-four hours didn't even pass, when the telephone rang, (guess who?) John couldn't help calling me at seven o'clock or talking to me at that hour of the morning. He used the excuse of the few things that I left at his home. Of course, they could have been picked up at any time. He didn't need to call for that special reason though his voice was a little different that morning. There had to be a reason for this. I hoped it wasn't anything bad, like bad news.

"John is there anything wrong? Your voice sounds a lot different than any other morning. You're not acting your normal self. What's the matter." I asked.

"Oh, it's nothing, Cathy. It's just the big let down from all the work we did in the last three years and that I would like to start on another project as soon as possible. When do we start?" He asked. (He has to be joking!)

"John, I like working with you and all, but remember what I told you the other night? That I would be taking some time for myself and the fact we have to let the heat blow over from what had happened last night? So people will not be talking about us. I do not like people talking about me like that. When it isn't true and even getting into the newspaper or the tabloids. Do you want that to happen? I said.

"No, of course not, but we are good for each other as far as working partners. That's all it is with me. What can they get out of that? Nothing. They can not get anything on us. Let them try!" he said.

"John be realistic. We have worked for three years together, without any space in between. I don't know about you, but I need time to get my thoughts together. I will be better person when I get back. If you want something to do, then why don't you try and see if you can get that project of making a reunion of "Dark Shadows" started and talk with the others. Since John knew the cast from the original "Dark Shadows and the script writer. It would be perfect project for him to do. Most of all I told him to take a vacation somewhere with his wife. They needed the time together alone without any kind of phone calls from anyone. I really had to give John a sales pitch. Neither one of us knew that Sharon was listening in on the extension. She agreed with me one hundred percent. Sharon wanted to have a second honeymoon of some kind. She was thinking about it for the longest time. John didn't know he was going to get another ear full from her too. It had worked out for the best for everyone concerned. Sharon and I had gotten what we wanted. On top of the list, was that well deserved rest.

I went to a travel agent, Tina. There was a moment I had to myself. The game plan was to get out of Los Angeles for three months to a place where I can meditate. It had to be a place that I was familiar with, somewhere where no one could find me. Tina suggested that I should go to London, England, then onto Paris, France and just travel Europe for those three months. It was a great idea, but it wasn't what I was looking for. I just wanted to stay in one spot for this trip. There was to much moving around when John wanted to look for the locations he wanted for this story of ours. Why just he couldn't just make up his own Paten Place. Everyone else does unless they been in this one little town that is just right for the scenery.

I told Tina, I wanted to go to Portland, Maine. I would need a rent-a-car. (National Rent a car,) and to stay at the "Comfort Inn" in Augusta for three weeks. I will find a spot to lay myself after that. Renting a room somewhere or even in someone's home. Tina wondered how I was going to do this and not knowing the area. She didn't know that I knew the area quite well for the last forty years. I told her there was no problem and that I would find my wary around and that I wouldn't get lost. Promising her that I wouldn't.

Once I got out of there. I stopped at Wal-Mart and got some things for the trip. It was one of those totes on wheels, like the Flight Attendants use for when they have to fly. I figured that I could get more things over there and hoped I wouldn't have to buy another suitcase or tote bag. The time there was going to be wonderful to be alone for awhile. It would be a well deserved rest.

The faster I got out of town, the faster I wouldn't have to answer the telephone and wondered of it would be John. I love to work, but there are limits to what I will do. Three years straight of nonstop work from one thing to the next. The days kept getting longer and longer by the day. There seemed to be no end to this, it went on and on. There was no end in sight. I couldn't take it anymore. The tension was getting to be to much. The stress and other things that combined with stress were building up in me. I never did something like this before. Sure, I would work an eight hour day and went home, but to be with someone all the time and do all of that work involve to getting down to the nitty gritty. A well deserved project and to have some time for myself. At least I have completed something in my life for once.

I quickly went home and put what I brought for the trip into the suitcase. I was raring to go. I called Matthew and told him that I would be out of town for three months and to keep an eye on my mother and to come and warm up the cars. He took the assignment, but told me that he would be gone for three weeks during the duration of time I was gone. It had changed a little. So I told him I would have to go to plan B then. Just go ahead and keep in touch with her as long as he could. Plan B was to call my aunt and see if Maxwell could come out for the summer and the fact he would get paid for his services when I came home from the trip. It would be an experience for him also. Maxwell needed to learn other things besides how to make parts.

I dialed the number to Continental Airlines and asked if they had a flight out later that day from Philadelphia to Los Angeles, (nonstop.) Jackie (the reservation agent,) had said that there were three of them. There was one at three-twenty and would arrive in Los Angeles at seven-twenty pacific time. I thought that was a little too close for comfort. The second one was at six-ten and would arrive in Los Angeles eight-twenty! That sounded a little better. I asked her about the third one. It would leave Philadelphia at ten thirty and would arrive in Los Angeles at nine-thirty. I didn't want Maxwell up at the airport at that hour of the night, by himself., though I would go meet him. I told Jackie that I would take the second one and hoped for the best. I gave her his name and call her back with my credit card number in a few minutes, because I wasn't sure if he could make it. She had reminded me that I had twenty-four hours to call back before they would cancel the reservation. I checked to see if she had put in the correct date. That he would be flying today and not tomorrow. Her reply was, "Oh, I'm sorry, your correct. I'm so use to saying it. A force of habit. I thanked her and hung up. Quickly I dialed my aunts number and just started praying that she was home and that Maxwell was there too. Someone picked up the receiver was my cousin Dexter. I asked if his mother was there. He replied by saying that she was and wanted to know what was going on? What was the emergency. There was no emergency of course, but I told him that he would find out in a few minutes, that I didn't want to be repeating myself a hundred times. The news was good news. He had nothing to be concerned about. He took that in a casual way.

I explained everything to my aunt Debbie and hoped that Maxwell didn't have a job somewhere or had other special plans for the summer. Her reply was, "No, he doesn't have a job as yet, but he is looking for one, though. Why do you ask?" "Because today is his lucky day. I do have a job for him. It is very simple. Maxwell will come and stay and house sit and to keep my mother company for three months or at least two and get paid well and he also can go to the places that you have seen already and then some. If he wants the fob, he better start packing as we speak and to pack lightly. Only one big suitcase. Just the basic clothes that he would wear during the week and a couple of Sunday best. With a jacket or sweater. Just like you did." I told her.

"When would you like him out there? Maxwell is jumping up and down like a jumping bean. He was so thrilled and honored." she said. "He better start packing now, because I have him on a flight out of Philadelphia at six-ten tonight that will arrive in Los Angeles at seven forty eight my time. The ticket will be paid for, so all you'll have to do is get to the airport and send him off on American Airlines flight number twelve. I will meet him at the airport, so that I do not have to give you any instructions and to waste any time here for the both of us. (I paused for a moment because I heard Maxwell in the background. He didn't know what the hell to do first. Dexter talked with him for a minute. To at least think of getting that one suitcase in the closet and just pack what he wanted to take. Then Debbie told him that she would be there in a minute to help him. Of course, Dexter wanted to get into the act too. He wanted to see if there was something for himself. The answer to that question was of course, no. With only one opening, I do not need two people for that job. Even Debbie wanted to get into the act. I don't know about those people. She just wanted to come out for the fun part of the trip. I think they were thinking of him flying alone. That it was his first trip on a plane and didn't know how he would react. The young man has to learn sometime. I just can't say no to one and yes to the other. I made a deal with her and she agreed with me. Debbie like that deal very much and of course wanted to come right away.

After I finished with my aunt, I called Continental Airlines to get the reservation for the trip back to Los Angeles, since I was passing through Newark anyway. I would pick her up there. It was some doing to get the reservations. I pulled it off somehow. Thank goodness that I knew the industry. I told her that she would have to fly from Philadelphia to Newark by herself, unless she had someone to take her to Newark. Debbie will just have to be brave for about forty minutes or so. She is use to traveling with someone or a group of people. For once she will just have to be independent for one hour and she wouldn't be traveling alone, with God, Jesus and the Holy Spirit, plus her guardian and the other passengers and the Flight Crew with her. I knew I didn't have nothing to worry about her flying alone.

Once that was settled. I could move on to something else. I checked my suitcase once again. I wanted to make sure that I had everything that I wanted. If there were things that I wanted or forgotten, I could get it over there. What was the sense of carrying it or wheeling it around! So happy that everything is going in the right direction and that there was no hang ups.

Busier than bee making honey, I was in fifth gear. If it wasn't one thing, it was something else. I got myself ready for the one-thirty flight. Thank goodness that I called Patrick and told him to be at the house at six-thirty. I had hired him for four hours, so that he could make the two trips to the airport. This was something that I wanted to do. Maxwell is a good kid and needed more opportunities in his life, besides what his father and grandmother were giving him. At least there would be one more expand to his horizon. An education that he wouldn't forget, not by a long shot. He had earned it in so many ways. Maxwell will never know what had hit him when he finally gets here.

By this time, I took a shower and gotten dressed and took the tote on wheels into the living room and waited a few minutes for Patrick to arrive. I called the Airlines to see if flight number twelve was on time and it was, thank God. The word was go has far as I was concerned. Seventh heaven was were I was at, at this point. Doing something nice for Maxwell and later on to bring my aunt back out here once again, because I knew she would want to see Dr. Robert Schuller at the Crystal Cathedral. I had to schedule it just right, because Dr. Schuller takes the summer off and I wouldn't have the time to take her over there before I had left and I didn't know if she would take one of the cars and just drive over there. I wouldn't want to be bothered with that now. Then the door bell rang, it was Patrick. He was right on time, which is good and that's what I like when I am looking for service of any kind. I had Patrick take my suitcase out to the car. I said my good-byes to my mother once again. She felt like we weren't spending that much time together and wanted some, but it had to wait till I came back from Maine. I truly needed my space.

On the way to the airport, I gave Patrick some instructions for once we get there and for on the way back. He agreed with them. We had no trouble getting to the airport, thank goodness. I had about twenty minutes to find out where the gate was and to get there in time for the plane. By chance, the plane was ten minutes early and I got there in the nick of time. The double doors opened. I waited right there. The time it took for the passengers to start coming out into the terminal. It felt like forever. It is always that way, when I want everything to go smoothly, then something usually happens, either a door of a plane is not cooperating, or it is late or something. It was just the plain fact that they were taking their time. Then one by one, the passengers started to come out. I kept an eye for Maxwell. Being his first time on a plane and being in Los Angeles, he might be in seventh heaven as well, just like his grandmother was in the past. Once the people did start coming out, it didn't take very long before I would find Maxwell, since I gave him a first class ticket. The kid was smart. He brought two duffel bags with all his stuff. I guess it was the quickest thing that they could find, instead of borrowing a suitcase from Auntie Em or anyone else and waste time or if that's the only thing that he had to use. It worked out for the best. We start to walk through the terminal. I started with the instructions and asking questions. Everything was moving right along. Just the way I like it. Once outside the terminal, I said, "Welcome to Los Angeles. This is the land of golden opportunities. What are you thinking, Maxwell?" (I waved my hand to Patrick to pull forward.) "Woo Wee, I can't believe it. Why did you just wave your hand and now that limousine is moving forward. What gives?" he said. "Just another thing that is used a lot out here, when you need or want one and with very little time involved here." (Everything was going as planned.)

Once we moved out of the airport, Maxwell was amazed and thrilled and honored to be out here and had thought that he would never have the opportunity to come out here, unless he had a job of some kind that brought him out here or just took a blooming vacation when he was sixty-five. His face was lit like a Christmas tree. The glow was so bright that we didn't need the headlights at all. On the way down I gave him his instructions and hoped that they had suck into his head somewhere. Even though he was saying yes, and oh yea. I even wrote it down and left it in the room that he was going to use after he comes down off of the cloud that he was on. I think that he was on a higher cloud than his grandmother was. It was the way he was acting. He was pretty amazed. He just couldn't believe that this was happening to him. Maxwell was really intrigued at all this. There was something for him, since he missed the first trip out here, that his grandmother had taken several years before. This is something special for him. I could see he was going to be something special. I just didn't want to break his bubble, but bubbles do get broken.

When we pulled up to the house, he was pretty spaced out. The house was surprising to him. To me, it was like any other house, but I think with Maxwell, he must of thought that it was a mansion. In a way, it was. It was roomy and plenty of space in each room. There was a room for every need you would want. My mother was at the front door. She wanted to help. There was no need to. Patrick put the two bags inside the door. I asked Maggie to take him into the kitchen and give him a cup of coffee or something to drink. I would call when I was ready to leave. I wasted no time. I took Maxwell to his room and gave him a grand tour of the house. Asking him if he had any questions. He had none.

That was good. It was very simple reminded him that under no circumstances should he tell his aunt anything about the arrangement that I had with him and that he was just here on vacation and that he wanted to see what his grandmother had seen and a lot more. His reply was, Ok, whatever you say. (Saying it with a big fat smile.)

I then rang the bell. That was to bring Patrick back into the picture. I was ready to leave and get started on my great adventure to Maine to be in isolation for awhile. It seemed to me I was being called there for some reason or another. I might seem like a long time to spend in another state for no apparent reason, but I knew what I was doing. There was very good reasons why I wanted to go to this lovely state. A person has to like the kind of life that they do have in Maine.

(1) Is because of the solitude.

(2) For the time away from the race.

(3) Is to get that Rest and Relaxation that I was looking for.

My plan will work. I know it will. I am just going there just for those reasons, I had just mentioned. There is going to be a lot of things I could do while I am there. First things first, I have to get there, right. I hoped for the best. Always doing something. That's little ole me.

By this time. The night was going quickly. One minute I was in Los Angeles and the next minute I was Newark. It was a peaceful flight and a peaceful night all around. I slept for three and a half hours, maybe a little longer. I sure needed it. The hour and a half in Newark was a fast one also. The whole experience was a breeze. There had to be a very good reason for this. Of course, at the time. I didn't know what the reason was. Merlin was in on the action. He was at my side once again. He wanted me to get to Maine safe and sound. (Merlin is my guardian angel.)

Everything was moving smoothly, too smoothly.

Usually something happens.

Like the time going very slowly.

Or getting some lip service from someone.

To the plane being delayed for an hour.

To people not cooperating with me.

To meeting someone that is grumpy.

To meeting someone that is a chatter box.

To someone that likes to just stair at you for no reason at all.

To any other reason that may come along. You name it, it usually happens to me.

Life is to short for things like this. No wonder I have lost a hundred and twenty pounds in the last three years. Meeting people like the ones mentioned a moment ago, to working so hard with John with the book and the script and getting the studio to make the movie, to finally getting it into the can. Sometimes I wondered when I did eat something. From day one, we were on the go from point A to point B. I can't ever remember when we took that ten minute break or a half an hour for lunch period.

Now I can just take it easy for three months, but also I have to deal with people that only care about themselves or they got up on the wrong side of the bed, to who knows what. I didn't really care either, if they didn't. When I walked on the plane and sat down where I belong. I had to the whole row to myself and just slept for that three and half hours or four hours. I was very happy for that. Thank God.

I was just eager to get to Maine and get three months of being a regular person once again. I was so happy I was doing this. I was glad that I knew the state of Maine the way that I do. Though I could of gone on that trip that Tina (the travel agent) was talking about, but I didn't want to be hopping around like a big bunny rabbit all over Europe. This bunny rabbit wanted to hop at a slower pace. Maine life was for me.

I'm hoping for the best. The way that it is going here now. It will be a wonderful three months after all, since everything was a green light from the word start. It will be my time in the bottle. Then when I went back to Los Angeles and John and I get back together as a team again. I am going to make sure that it is not going to be three years before taking my next vacation. I will guarantee you that for sure. I will not stand for it. Or the airlines taking their time getting everyone on board the plane or one of the employee's giving me a hard time. (They must think that they are something else or that they shit doesn't smell.) I dislike people like that. Whatever happened to the customer is always right. Just because they have a job that they like and have the right stuff., they don't need to take it out on the customer, they wouldn't be in business. Or some other passenger thinks that he or she is more important than the next guy. I don't care who you are, you maybe important in your job, (whatever it is,) but you're no better than the next person. Just because you have made your marked in life in whatever occupation. That's great if you did, but you don't have to take it out on the little guy or someone that is making their mark in life or is trying too.

Before I knew it, I was in Portland, Maine. I got up from the seat I was sitting in and walked down the isle and picked up my tote on wheels and walked off the plane and kept on trucking until I got to the rent-a-car place.

"Yes, may I help you, madam?" said Donna.

"Yes, you can. I am Cathy. I have a reservation for a full size car!" I told her. (While Donna looked in her computer for me. I looked in my purse for the check I was going to give them.) Within minutes, everything was taken care of.

Now, it was time to go off and see the wizard. I just had one more leg to this trip. Once more hour to go, before getting to my final destination. I was feeling so great, even though I was traveling all night and had only gotten four hours of sleep. I have done this kind of thing before. It gets a little easier each time. It wasn't the fact I had to be there at a certain time, for a business meeting of some kind, but when you want to get the hell out of town the fastest way. When you are stressed out and just wanted to do something different or just get away from it for while, even if its for two weeks or a month. I just picked three months. Since I was working freelance and it has been awhile since I took a break like this. I am the type of person that needs to get away from it all every once in awhile. I can't just keep on going like some people do. They are the ones that are missing out on seeing what is out there and will not accomplish anything. Sure, they might get the mighty dollar, but you can't take it with you, and could die at the ripe old age of forty-eight of a heartache. That's not for me. I want to live to the ripe old age of ninety.

With the radio on and thinking about what I would like to do, once I get into the greve of the Maine life. I will be so happy. Before I could say super-calagigies-exbedale-a-doses, I was near the off ramp to Augusta. I did the speed limit. I just wondered how it could be possible. That an hour could go so quickly. Within moments, I was at the "Comfort Inn in Augusta. I quickly parked the car. I checked in and got into the room I was assigned to. All I wanted to do, was to stretch out onto the bed and just lay there for awhile. It is hard being in a sitting position for a little over nine hours. The bones in your body tend to get stiff in some places. I am not complaining, mind you, but it is worth every pain and discomfort I have, just to be here. It is worth it to me. There are times, when a person has to just get away from it all and do something that they truly want to do. It could be very simple. Look deep into your heart. Take the time to explore those adventures that you may want to do. Why just make the mighty dollar and don't use it for that special something. Whether it is that grand vacation to who know where, to getting that special kind of car that you always wanted all these years! Just go for it. Life is to short as it is.

Three months may sound like a lot of time for a vacation, but when you are stressed out like I was, three months is not enough. At first, I didn't know how to act, being so use to getting up and just going to work. I know there is more to life than that. This area was so familiar, that I knew it like the back of my hand. The question that I had at the moment was. "Where do I begin this holiday of my own dream world?" I knew it was only my first day and all, but when you are coming off of a very fast roller coaster and get down to a speed that is the right speed or even slower, it is not easy at all. Going from speedy gonzales to the life of Reilly was the trick. For the reminder of the day, I had taken it easy. The plan was just to relax my whole body from all the tension by meditation. It was the only way I could chill out. If it works, why knock it. I was so glad to get out of Los Angeles that it wasn't even funny. It wasn't the work and working with John, but working day and night, and working like crazy.

Lets say that you were driving down this road and in the distances you seen a man standing were you see the gravel. Would you go and see this man with the Golden Robe on. Or would you make that left hand turn right there and just go back to home base. And for the rest of your life you would be wondering why? So I could help a friend.

Would you stay in your car or would you get out of the vehicle and get a little closer so you could see it more clearly what this man was going to show you. To hear what Merlin said about this whole thing and to go on with life until you heard a word. One simple word that could change everything. It is "<u>LIGHTHOUSE.</u>"

That was the key to this whole thing. Even John didn't even realize that until I brought it to his attention, and with the help of Sharon (his wife,) they are on the other side of the world. John and Sharon were already in the Caribbean on their second honeymoon. They were having a grand ole time. They hadn't been together is so long, that it was like they were starting all over again. John mad the connection with what I was talking about and what Sharon told him. (In general, it was basically what I was trying to tell him.) Then he could go and work on another project or two. As long as she had some time with him, that's all she was asking for. Or even to work on a project with him. I hope that didn't mean that she was getting a little jealous there. I certainly hope not.

Meanwhile, back in the states. I laid down for a little bit. My body was so relaxed that it had needed some rest from somewhere. (So I thought.) What I didn't know was, Merlin had something to do with it. He wanted to show me something. Isn't that always the way? Just when you want to get into the swing of things, someone wants to show you something else that has nothing to do with what you want to do, or tell you something that is so impotent to them, when half the time, it isn't so great after all. But with Merlin, it was important. It only took him a couple of minutes to tell me.. It was like I was in a daze of some kind. Then I closed my eyes. I began to see some different colors, going around and around, then at the very tip of the circle of colors, it started to open up and I could see something forming. It was out in the country, near by. Zooming in on the location. It was at the head of Parker Lake. I saw a man standing there. He looked familiar. Who is he? What is his name?

"Hello Cathy, You are wondering what is going on and who I am. Don't you remember? We have met before. I am the one that brought your grandfather to you. I am your guardian angel, Merlin. I want you to look at the lake. See how peaceful it is? There is something I would like you to see. (The water was like ice.) It will happen very soon. You will not remember this when you wake up, only when things started happening. That's when you'll remember. Please do not take this on a personal level. It was meant to happen anyway." said Merlin.

When I looked at the lake, the water and forest were so peaceful. It was like the right before Christmas, not a stir anywhere. The stage was set. Act one was ready to start any moment now. I just wondered what Merlin had to show me that was so important. Of why it couldn't wait until I went over there. I guess he couldn't wait till I got over there, either later on that day or that very next morning. What was the rush? Maybe it was the best way that he could tell me and the fact I wouldn't remember it, until the time comes.

The scene opened up on the freeway, going west bound on the ninety-one. There were cars going to their destinations. This one car belonged to John and Sharon. They were on their way to Las Vegas. John knew one of the people that were up there (he wanted to see.) This was after he had contacted someone else to find his location. The speedometer was reading fifty-five miles an hour. There was no rush to get there. Then all of a sudden, the window shattered, on the passengers side. There was a bullet. It went right into Sharon's neck and missed a vital organ. John took the next off ramp, because he saw a sign that said "Hospital" next exit. He didn't remember the name of the hospital, but knew exactly where it was located. He gone as fast as he could. He was even thinking, "Where are the police, when you need them?" John pulled up to the emergency room door. A nurse was on her break. He asked her to get him some help and that his wife was shot. She went into the door and there was a stretcher right there. The nurse brought it out as fast as possible. No matter what anyone had did for her, it wasn't the bullet that would kill her, it would be human error. Within an hour at the hospital, Sharon was dead. John was beside himself. He wondered how this could of happened. He reacted in a rage. He loved her so much. They took him into one of the other rooms to subdued him and to get him to sleep it off. That wasn't going to do the trick. He was going to do something about this. I just knew this for a fact. Inside him was this fury that will not quit. He will fight to the bitter end. John was that way. He knows when he wants out of life. In due time, he went to court and won twenty million dollars in a practice suit against the doctors and the hospital. It may not bring his wife back, but in her memory he will do something with the money.

This is were the vision ended. "Go my child and make the difference. John will need you in the future. He will need all the support that he can use. You will be that great help for him, when the time comes. When you wake, you will not remember. On the word, "<u>Lighthouse</u>" that's when you'll remember. It will be a hard fight to the end, but you will get through the ordeal and John will get the education of a life time. You will be a better person, because of it, too. Then everything started to disappear. I, continued to sleep until I was ready to wake up.

It was like a total dream to me. The three months I was in Maine, went as fast as the road runner. Sure, there was plenty of meditation and rest, also I did a lot of other things, but why did three months feel like three days? Good question.

By the time the plane was landing in Los Angeles. My aunt and I went out to the curb, and waited for the airport bus. Within moments the bus pulled up to the curb, the one that was going to Disneyland. I guess Debbie (my aunt) was still in seventh heaven. She acted like she did the first time. She still couldn't believe that she was here and that she wanted more of what we had. I guess with some people it takes more than a few times to get over that certain hill or mountain. I knew that she was honored and all, but Debbie was glowing from ear to ear.

At least on this trip, I had all the time with her, instead of someone trying to cut into the piece of the action and try to take some of that time away. When this person can see you at anytime back home, more than the person their visiting. People should realize that when they are in someone else's home and they are not a member of the family and they were invited to come along for the ride to keep the other one company. Plus the fact that they know the person is visiting at a great distance. They should be allowed to visit with the people that they come to see. One of the hostess should not be treated like she was a servant.

We got into the swing of things that California has. Since Debbie was going to be there longer than a week and more than two. We just took it easy that day. Though she did want to do something, but I told her that a lot of places want reservations of some kind. I made her realize that there is a time difference and she had to get use to it, since she is not use to traveling by aircraft to get her somewhere quicker. Though there were places that I could have taken her, I didn't want to do anymore for that one particular day, because I was so relaxed and mediated out. I had to get into the swing of things myself.. I gave her the grand tour of the house instead. Debbie was satisfied with that.

Life is strange, one day you can be as poor as poor can be and the next day you can be a millionaire with forty-eight million dollars. That's one hell of a blow, don't you think? Isn't it?

By Sunday morning, it was five forty-five in the morning. I got up. I knew that this day was going to be a very special day at the Crystal Cathedral. This was no ordinary Sunday. To me, it was nothing to see all the different celebrates or in seeing Dr. Robert Schuller the first. But for my aunt it was a big deal to her, to finally see him in person, instead of on television, with the "Hour Of Power" that was something for her. Not only that, it is also stepping into the church itself. It changes you somehow. It talks to you. My aunt was a changed woman. She was more spiritual. More with one called Jesus Christ. The Lord Jesus gave her more strength and to be more independent. She wouldn't be afraid of anything. After the service so told me that she wanted to join the Crystal Cathedral. I told her that it would take six weeks course and that she would have to stay out here for that duration of time. Debbie didn't care,

43

all she wanted was to join and be a part of this great church. So I told her that I would have to find out for her the information that she needed. Today was her lucky day. That following Sunday, they were going to start another class. She signed up for it. Everything was handled beautifully.

The time came and went. We were so happy to have the time together and for her to graduate from the Crystal Cathedral that the sky was the limit. We could challenge anything or anyone, at this point. Debbie didn't want to go home, when it was time to go. It would be to boring back in her neck of the woods. She went like a good little girl. With all that she had to tell the family and her friends, it will take her awhile for her to explain it to everyone.

With all the commotion with my aunt. I received a message from John that he and Sharon were heading out of town. To talk with one of the cast members of the original "Dark Shadows" and see if her would consider doing the reunion. They were off to the <u>lighthouse</u>. That brought me the clue that I needed for what Merlin told me. By this time that I could call them, they had already left. I was told by the housekeeper. Isn't that always the way.

I grabbed my purse and jumped into my mustang. I quickly go onto the ninety-one freeway east bound. I wasn't quick enough. Since they had a head start on me. Merlin was right. I just wondered why. They were a loving couple and so forth. I just kept going. I went to the exit and got off. I made a left hand turn, then a mile down the street I made a right hand turn. Within moments, I was at the hospital that I was shown. I parked the car and (I saw the car and the window was shattered and blood was all over the place.) I turned and walked into the emergency room. The room was empty, so there wouldn't be any problem looking for John. He wasn't there. I went up to the nurses station and asked the nurse where John Black was. Sherry had no idea were he was and why I wanted him. I asked her to go in the back, because he may not come through this station. It was important that I find him. She got up from the chair that she was in and went into the back and checked what they had. I also gave her the name of his wife. Thank goodness that I did go, maybe that was what I was suppose to do. I was grateful that I didn't get one of those nurses that were so high and mighty and maybe their jobs went to their heads and asks you every question in the book, when it wasn't necessary. I dislike these kinds of people. I even lied to her and told her that I was John's sister.

Sherry (the nurse) came back. She asked me to follow her into the back. I was glad that they did, so that I knew what the hell was going on and to be with John. By the time they got me there. They were moving Sharon. They wanted a few x-rays of the area. Apparently they had just gotten there. They wanted to make sure that it wasn't near anything vital or would damage anything. Sue (another nurse) asked us to wait in their waiting room, that it would be another few minutes. That will be the day when it is only a few minutes. It will be a few hours will be more like it. I just know these things, that's all.

Merlin's prediction came true. I just wanted to know why this had to happen to a very nice couple. Sharon had done nothing to deserve something like this. She was a very good person. Why do the good have to either die very young or something happens to them that is so horrible. Then the ones that are wicked live to a ripe old age of ninety and have nothing wrong with them. I will never understand something like that. It will take a lot of explaining for me to understand all this.

The night was long and busy there for awhile. John had to stay the night, because he was getting out of control and they just wanted to watch him. That he doesn't do anything foolish. The doctor ordered something that had made him sleep the whole night through. That was some strong medication. I think that it could knock out an elephant. By morning, when John woke up, I was right there beside his bedside. I explained everything to him of what had happened. It seemed that he had some hangover. It was from the medication.

Once we got out of there. John got his car phone. He called his lawyer and set up an appointment so that he could get a lawsuit started. He already notified the hospital and the doctors that they were going to be sued. It's not easy to go through something like that. It take so much energy and time to go through this. All the time it takes, especially if the other party in question is giving all kinds of trouble and trying to get the hell out of it. They were not going to get away with it. They even tried to pay John a smaller amount of money so that they wouldn't have to go to court, but John wasn't going for any out of court settlements. He went the whole nine yards.

In the duration of the three years that it took John to get the case solved. We formed a relationship both in business and on a personal level. I didn't want to go that far, but it did. Things just developed. We did a lot of things together. We took a lot of trip and got that one project off the ground, called "Dark Shadows Reunion" or was just about finished with it.

Once John got the settlement from the hospital and the doctors for twenty million dollars each. We set a date for our wedding and we married. It was a small wedding. Just a few close friends and Tracy and June and their husbands weren't invited to the wedding and we lived happily ever after.

Though Cathy and John are happily on their way to a heavenly experience. Would you like to have some peace of mind? Then I suggest to you that you find something that would make you happy. Take that break from those test tubes, or those lesson plans, to looking at those blue prints, to take a vacation somewhere and just relax. Who knows what you may think of when you in that relaxed state. To go forward with those plans into action. Just don't sit there and say to yourself, "What if I became a _____. You fill in the blank.

1. What do you think, now?

_____

_____

_____

_____

2. Is it a WOW!! YES OR NO.

3. Are you going to do something a little differently? YES OR NO.

4. Would you take the challenge like Cathy and John had, if it ever happened. YES OR NO.

5. Did you think of something that you could be doing, instead of what you are doing right now?

YES OR NO!

6. What will it be, hot dogs and beans or be a steak and lobster? Your choice!

For you vegetarians, eggs and toast or some gourmet meal? Your choice!

7. What are you going to do now?

_____

_____

8. Are you going to stay where your at or not? YES OR NO!

Cathy Ann

THIS IS THE STAGE THAT IT WILL HAPPEN ON. AN EXPERIENCE FOR ANYONE TO GO THROUGH IF THEY NEVER WENT THROUGH AN EXPERIENCE LIKE IT BEFORE. THIS IS YOUR STAGE. YOU WILL SEE A PLAY THAT IS SO INCREABLE. IT MAY NOT BE PUT INTO WORDS THAT YOU COULD DESCRIBE IT. IT IS SOMETHING OUT OF THE ORDINARY A PLAY THAT DOESN'T HAPPEN EVERYDAY. SEE WHAT YOU THINK ABOUT THIS WHOLE THING!

Chapter Five
The Show Of Shows

Have you ever taken the time to just sit there and just stair into space? Have you ever thought of something in one particular way of how it would have happened if it happened in this order? I wondered what it would be like if it would happen in a way that you may not of thought of. Or just let your imagination go let it be free for a change. On the other hand, are you afraid of letting go? Afraid of finding something out. Is that the answer that you have for me? There is nothing to fear expect fear itself. Find your truth. Let your mind go out there. Even to explore your own mind, if necessary. But let something happen. Find your goal and deal with it. Be at peace with yourself. When in doubt, just think about it. Let you mind be free and explore what you need to find out. Let whatever come out. Don't be afraid, despite what it is.

As the scene opens up, looking at Parker Lake, in the town of Mt. Vernon, Maine. It is a quaint little town. With the water calm as ice and the trees as green as they will ever be. The flowers and the bushes as lovely as they do in the spring. With all the buildings surrounding the lake on the different parts as far as the eye can see, from the point of origin. It looked like a masterpiece that a painter would put on his canvas. A place that you would see in the movies somewhere. It was real and is. Or was as if you would walk onto the water as Moses would have, if he could.

It was an early Monday morning. I (Cathy) walked down to the ledges to look at this photograph. I was shocked and surprised myself. That this event was for me or those things do happen like this. The water was so clear. I thought at first that they water was like ice and I could walk to the other side, (even with my weight of two hundred and fifty pounds, but I didn't.) It was about five forty-five in the morning. As I looked over to my right side. I saw the fog rolling in onto the lake. It was setting itself up like there was a film or stage crew setting the stage for a play or movie. Getting those valuable things in the right places. I could not believe my eyes. It was too early in the morning for any tricks. I thought that I could have been dreaming or was fantasizing all this! I could not believe it as if anyone else would have either that would have been there. Thank goodness that I was alone to see the, because I do not know what John or Jane Doe would have done. I wiped my eyes and opened then again, but still it was doing the same thing. Making the different shapes and moving closer. It had gotten thinner as it go closer to me. Then everything stopped. I did not know what to expect. I had no fear. I was going to see this through. It felt there would be an important message there for me. There was something to all of this. I knew that for sure.

The play was about to begin. I was ready for what may come. Who knows what this play will turn out to be? There were many questions going through my mind. I would like to know what this was all about. On the other hand, what this all meant? What strange things could happen now? What does it mean? Good questions, I think. What do you think?

A man of sixty-six years young came out onto the stage. He had this golden robe on. His hair was all white. Very good looking for a man of his age. His eyes were brown, his built was tall, and broad shoulders and weighted hundred and ninety pounds. Someone I would not mind going out with or just meeting the man. He walked to the spot to begin this whole thing. Merlin (the man) must have been the master of ceremonies.

'Good Morning to one and all. I am glad that you could come to this production. This is just for your eyes only

Cathy. I am Merlin. I am your guardian angel. You have many angels working for you, but I am your main one you can call upon. I know that your life has not been easy, up until now, but you can start doing something about it now. Why don't you do the most important thing you like to do? Why don't you start small and then you may get somewhere with the book. The one you call "Born Too Late". It is a very good of you to work for those five years on it and had worked hard all these years to get it just right and to the way you like it. Plus, to share it with the people, you have already, but you need to no nationwide with this. Your plan did not work for you did it? Or did you just think that you could have sold some of them to the other people while you were here and just sent them a copy? I do not want to break your bubble, but with this group, I do not think so. Lay low for awhile. Your time will come my good woman.

It is time for you to see someone that you have not seen in sometime. A man that you loved for a long time ago and you had thought you had killed. In which you did not. It was not your fault. You did not know. It was not your fault. You may talk with him now Cathy. Your grandfather has waited this long to talk with you too. He has things to say to you also. Thomas Marks would you please come out onto the stage. You need to take your position." said Merlin.

I could not believe what was happening. I could not believe what I was seeing or hearing. A man that says that he is your guardian angel. And that I should not being doing "Born Too Late" first and I should be doing something else first. Every time I write something it turns out to be a long story. What should I do? I cannot write an article or a short piece, but I will give it an old school try. Maybe he will lead me after I go home to California, because I am not getting anything here and with my mother here, is no help. With her talking all of the time and following me around as if I was going to do something special without her. I do need my own space. If a person thinks that another person is going to do something, then they will. Then there are some that don't. For an example, if you think that someone wants their own space, because they may go out there and have something to eat. Just because they are on the heavy side. That's not always the case. It may be the fact of this person not being busy enough. Not to go and have two hamburgers somewhere and then come back and eat whatever the meal is. That's not my bag. There is no trust anywhere. I am only specking for myself. I do not like to be spied on. Or someone to try to fit in and they don't. There are many time you cannot be apart of everything. The only person or spirit that should know everything is the Lord Jesus and His Father.

I looked over to where my grandfather was standing. He looked the same to me, as I remembered as a child. A man that was five-eight, the gray wavy hair, these funny looking glasses the he wears. The casual clothes he always like to put on. The smile upon his face all the time. Always warm and loving. Someone I hope to find, if I ever gotten serious about anyone. Someone I could do anything with. Of course with my grandfather, it was up to a point. A bond between us that will never be broken. He was always there for me, whether he was dead or alive. I could feel him there. I never told anyone.

I am glad to see you and the fact that I can talk with you. It is not going to be a one sided this time. I know that you want to do some talking yourself and your sorry. I just wished it never happened the way it did. There is no love lost there. I really tried to tell you and also about the other things that were happening around you. The wall must have been thick that the communication did not go through on my part. I heard you clearly. We will be seeing a lot of each other. I will grant you that. I will be your knight in shinning armor. Through Merlin, you can set up the dates that you would like to talk with me. Only if it is important. Write this for the first piece. Tell everyone of the experience, whether other people believe it or not. I will help you with some of the stories. I have so much to say to you, my little angel. Just remember that it was not your fault. It was meant to be, since things turned out the way they did. It hurts, I know. When it is time for you to join us here in heaven. There we will have plenty of time to be with each other. I do not want to take anymore time at this point. I love you, Cathy. Remember me. You will have a lot going for you, very soon. Do not give up the ship. Do what your heart feels. Do what you always wanted to do, ever since you were sixteen. Do not listen to others. They are jealous that you have these stories in you. (They wished that they could have written it themselves.) You will be famous, because of it. Believe me, my child. I know that it takes you time to do what you have to do. That is why you should start now. It will be easier down the road. They will be more frequent, and then they are now. Trust me, Cathy." said the grandfather.

Then Thomas stopped talking. His time was up for the moment. He just stood there like a robot. It was so odd to see him like that. There was nothing that I could do. I was not the one in control. I had to go with the program. Marlin must have had other things to do or to show me. I wondered what was going to be next. Everything was at a stand still. However, the show went on as planned.

"Cathy, my child. Thomas is right. He will be at your side. Along with me. I know that you love your grandfather so much and do not like to see him like this. You must think that he is a robot or just something that I am controlling. It will be different the next time that you see him. He will be a spirit, a light and you will know by his voice the it is he. Then from this point on, he will be that spirit, he will not be able to come to you anytime that you would like him to come. You will be busy with other things that you will be doing. I cannot tell you much. The decision will be yours when the time comes for them. You have to chose. You can make the right ones. Like a vacation in England, and to Sydney, Australia. Good idea to go. Go for the gold and nothing less. There are some other people that I could like for you to see. Some of them you have admired for years. You will know them on sight." Said Merlin.

Then the people that Merlin told me about started to come onto the stage. It was as they were going to do a play for me. First, I could not believe seeing all those people. Whether they were dead or alive, and that I would meet some of these people in the future. They would play in one of my books that I wrote. It took a few minutes for them to come onto the stage. They all looked like robots. A very blank face, stiff as a board, no feeling about them. I do not know why things had to be like this, but I was not the one in control.

"What's the matter, Cathy? Is there something wrong?" said Merlin.

"I think you know what I am going through and what my first question would be. Why are these nice people like this? Why do they have to look like robots or like they do? It does not look like they are spirits or ghost at all. Just something that looks like a person. Why is that may I ask? (I stared at him, until I got the answers I wanted to know. I was not going to take any answer.)

"Now Cathy, don't be afraid at all. I thought that it would be best if they did come out this way and could talk with anyone you would like to talk to. It may not be all of them, but with a couple of them. I had no idea that this would effect you in this way. I did not know at all. I knew that these people are great people in their own right. I do care. I am not inhuman, you know. I can love just like you do to your grandfather. I am not inhuman. Talk with a couple of them. Just believe me that this is not hurting them in any way, trust me!!" said Merlin.

"I guess, I'll have to, since you're from Heaven. I know that you are not from the devil. A friend told me of you. She had given me a good description of you and that you were my guardian angel. What's next?" I asked. "Talk to anyone that you wish!!" he said. (He moved his arm as he was turning.)

"May I go up to whomever it is and talk with them face to face or could they come to me, instead?" I asked. "Either way you like!" he said. (He had this look upon his face, that I could do anything, at this point.)

I know that I could not walk on the water, so each one of them came to me. If there words, I spoke to that person. There were a few that I did not care for they turned my stomach for some reason. As each of them left, they went out the same way that they came in. It was like being in school and having a drill of some kind. All lining in a straight line and when it was time for them to leave, then had exited the same way. Even Merlin went out one of the exits. The fog started to disappear. I was in a kind of shock, I guess. This was unbelievable. There was no telling what was going to happen next. Is this my imagination? Did the play really happen? Good question, don't you think? I did not tell the other at the place I was staying at. I can hear them now. That it was my imagination or was it a dream of some kind? That it would be great for one of my stories of mine. I did not need that. I wanted people to start believing me when I say things like this. No matter how incredible it may seem. I am the one that saw it and I could not believe it either. So how could I expect someone else to believe it. Time will tell. With some of the things, that Merlin told me about some of the people that were there. I could not believe it myself. They were great in what they did. No matter what part they played. From Burt Lancaster, Lawrence Olivier to

Boris Karrloff. And it goes on and on. There were so many of them.

I gotten up from the chair I was sitting in and went back to my cabin before someone found me. I did not want them to start asking the sixty-four thousand dollar questions. When I have to go to number eight and went into my room I was in, I found my shell of a body. Was this a dream? Did I see what I saw? Or did I have an out of body experience and didn't even know it. Went on as if nothing happened.

Life is funny sometimes. A person can get help from most anywhere. Not just from your friends and relations, but their guardian angel. Why at this time? Did Merlin do this? That was my question! To get me moving in the right direction. To get the ball rolling. I do not know, but I also got the same information from a woman that teaches at one of the colleges or universities here in Maine. Did Merlin tell her the same thing? Or was it by chance, that she would have told me these very same facts. It was up for grabs. I will go that route and see where that takes me. I hope that I do not get the million and on layoff notices as I did with the publishers (to sell my book.) The first one I would like to get out there is "<u>Born Too Late</u>". As I said before. When this woman had to go through up until nineteen ninety is so incurable. I could not believe what she was telling me, without any description of any kind, (of the people in the story, so that I could check her story out.) Not wanting to tell the world what anyone looked like, because she did not want to give the main charter (male charter) away. Though I wouldn't have put Sam's description in there either, but on the other hand, she could have made a whole lot of difference, even if it was made up. That is the way that she wanted it to be. I guess. However, it is one hell of a story.

After truly waking up from a sound sleep and went into the bathroom. I went and sat down in one of the chairs on the porch. I had a whole month of this. I figured that why should I go and lye down for a very short time. I was wide awake by this time. I think that there was a reason for this, but didn't know what it was at the time, that Merlin got my interest and that is the reason why I couldn't go back to sleep. Plus, seeing my grandfather and the other people that were there, on the lake. I had something to look forward when I got home. Something that was in my memory locked. Not knowing that I was getting some stories while I was there. I thought I locked out. The week of Labor Day was a different story. I was working like a little trooper. With Labor Day with this story. And for the rest of the week was, "Something Too Remember".

I give my thanks to "Bearnstow" and to Alice Ann Bloom. Maybe I needed that answer after all. I was so glad that I did give a copy of "Born Too Late" to Alice Ann. It paid off in so many ways. I may not of gotten any money out of it yet, but the information would be like a pot of Gold. So is this what a writer has to do to start from the bottom. Before getting their big break, a person lives and learns all the time, no matter who you are. No matter what kind of personality you have, you can be stubborn as a mule or a person like me that wants a lot of input. Life is too short not to learn a little thing like where you put those important papers. You cannot always have your aid with you. Look, it took me a whole month and a lot of money and to go thirty-four hundred miles to get this information. I just hope that this does the trick that will do it for me. I am just hungry to get out there and see how the public likes my stories, they are somewhat different, more down to earth. Even this was a dream or prediction of what may happen to me the next time that I go to "Bearnstow", it may have been an out of body experience and I didn't know it. At least I am heading in the right direction, (I hope.) The place is real. The act was not a dream.

This is not made up. This was not my imagination or anything else that you may think of. Where did it come from if it didn't come from my imagination? Give a thought for a moment. Which is the most logical?

Thanks again to Alice Ann Bloom and to Ruth Grauert.

Imagine if you were in this woman's shoes and going on a journey for God.

1. What do you of it now?

2. What did you get out of it?

3. How would you rate this (From one to hundred.)

4. Would you like to give it as a gift to someone?

5. Would you recommend this to another person?

6. How do you feel now that you have read this story?

You can use another piece of paper, if you like to. So you could keep you book intercede.

Chapter Six

A Lost Little Lamb

What could a person do, if they are a lost little lamb? What if they have been looking for a place for so many years, and all along it was right in their own backyard, and didn't even know it. It could be tapping them right on their shoulder and have done it so many times. It isn't easy trying to find a church. It is like trying to look for anything, from a good doctor, dentist, a car repair person, to looking for a church. You don't know who to trust, until you get to that right place, where they will not be those kinds of people where they will not take an arm and a leg. That also means a church. Since in recent years, with people in the church going in the wrong direction. So where could a lost little lamb Trusting in Jesus and in God, along with the Holy Spirit, but the house of worship was the key.

I (Cinderella) have been in a situation like this, of being a lost little lamb. I always thought that so long as you believed in Jesus Christ and in God, that it didn't really matter. I did my prayers and tried to be good. I have known this for the last sixteen or seventeen years that I have been in California, that I've been unhappy when I went to church. It was the church that I was going to. It got so bad, that I only went twice a year, (Easter and Christmas,) or when we had company which wasn't that often, thank goodness, because the minister at the place of worship was a real bore, and thought that he was something else and went a little to over board with some of his actions. (At first, it was nothing bad, but always showing up at dinner time and expected something to eat, until the people had got wise to him in that department. Plus asking the families that had money, for some of it all the time, for this and that. That's no good. Just because he was single and loves to spend money. (Why doesn't he use the peanut brain of his and think of things to raise the money.) Thank God, that he was only there for ten years, that's long enough. He got caught and was fired.

Enough of that. My life wasn't an easy one. Always taking anything so that I could survive. There was something there telling me that I wasn't satisfied. That I should be doing something a whole lot different than what I was doing. I was living in New Jersey and moved back to the land of California. This is where I felt comfortable. I want to feel comfortable.

In nineteen ninety. I had a wish come true. A wish or dream come true. My aunt Barbra was planning a trip with her two daughter, (Sue and Betsy), but for some reason or another, they told their mother, that they couldn't come. I wished that they had come, instead of the woman that did come with her. If Barbra was going to pay for her ticket, then why didn't she just bring one of her grandson, Dennis. He would have been a lot better than her girlfriend, but Barbra knows now, that she did make a mistake, because she was told a little over a year later, after the incident had happened by myself and Sue.

But before that ever happened. When it was getting down to the nitty-gritty of her flight out here to California. I asked her for the flight information. So that I wouldn't get a knock at the door, at seven o'clock in the morning and it would be them. Though, when I got the information and when I touched the envelope, and the sheet of paper, I felt something. I felt something was going to happen. I didn't know what was going to happen. I just started praying like crazy. I asked the LORD Jesus to please intervene and help out. Maybe to stop what was going to happen, or to help Barbra get to a point to where she could leave the situation and hoped that my feelings weren't about her not coming, but other things. Unfortunately, something did happen. If only my uncle David didn't died two years before this. He was with us whether anyone believed me or not. He was there!!! Because I felt his spirit with us when my aunt did finally arrive here in Los Angeles. Before I get into that, I just wanted to mention this. It was in the middle of July when I received the letter I was waiting for, from my aunt Barbra with the flight information. I wish I never asked her for it. I had this warm sensation or feeling from the paper and the envelope that something was going to happen. I hoped that it was a situation where she could get out of, so that she could take the trip. I hoped that the situation wasn't about her. The six weeks were something else. I was on pins and needles. Always afraid she was going to cancel over the phone. I was close to a nerves break down. It was right on the edge, but I pulled through, by the skin of my teeth. I was so relieved, when I saw her walking off of that plane. The week went fast.

On the Tuesday before Barbra and her girlfriend left, I knew that she would want to go to see the Crystal Cathedral. We took them over there. It was a real honor for all of us. I didn't think anything of it, at the time. A church is a church. The only difference is the minister and the way the church is built. It took another five years before I became a member. It took God, Jesus and the Holy Spirit to get me there. They all thought they needed something or someone that would get me inside the church. It would have to take something real special or someone of great importance. To get me over there. While I was away on business, Martha, (my mother) found a full page advertisement in the newspaper, that Roger Williams was going to be there for one night only. She went ahead and got two tickets. We, both went that night, that he was there and it did the trick. The next morning I called the church and asked for membership. I talked with Frances. For at least twenty minutes. I signed up I took the class and graduated December 17, 1995.

I did hear my calling to go over there, but with all the different things that were going on at the time. Some people use the pulpit to make their money, so they could have two or three homes (million dollar ones, no less,) to having all kinds of cars and all kinds of things. I didn't want to mixed up with something like that. No wonder I didn't want to be bothered.

Now I have found my new home and I am loved and needed by others. It feels great to be in that position. I never felt that way before, and that one of these days I am going to be doing something as special for the Crystal Cathedral. I know what it is, but rather not say until the day that I can do it. It is something very surprising for Robert Schuller and the congregation. I don't want to give it away. I'm not going to tell.

You see, when you look for something, it is usually right in your own backyard. The bit comes up and bites you, if you're not careful.

Cathy Ann

Chapter Seven
What Is Sixteen Tons And A Barrel Of Fun?

What is life anyway? Is it suppose to be about problems and worries and wonders what you're going to be doing next, with this problem or that one? Or are you going to deal with the problem right up front. What is going to be your answer? My answer would be deal with the problem right up front. It won't go away until you deal with it. You may turn to something else, but it only cause other problem that you'll have to deal with in the future. So think before you go and do something foolish to solve one problem and end up with another problem, that could be a lot worse than the original problem. It could be a lot harder to stop the second problem then the first problem, in the first place. Why put more on our shoulders then we already have, and make it sixteen tons?

Life is too short to be worrying about this problem that most Americans have. There are many problems that we have here in America with the drugs, violence, drive by shootings and who knows what. Sure, all the problems need to be solved, but we will start right in your own home. Deal with yourself for a change. Give yourself a boost. You're always thinking of others, why not think of yourself, in dealing with the one problem that you may have had for a couple of months or a couple of years. It may be a lot longer for some people.

This writer is talking about your weight problem. Even if you only have twenty to thirty pounds or the real extreme of being a hundred, a hundred and fifty, to three hundred pounds overweight. Sure, it's easy to talk about doing it, but to get on this track to start is the hardest for anyone, including myself.

I know what you maybe thinking. "Sure, there is Jenny Craig, and Weight Watchers and other programs that are out there, but I can't afford those programs. Or, I don't have the time to go through a program like theirs. You can say that to me. Please don't use this as your excuse. You are wasting valuable time, in getting started. I could do the very same thing of telling you those excuses, but why should I waste our valuable time.

It is hard getting over that hump or that mountain to get started. If you don't do it, then no one is going to do it for you. Give a try and don't tell me that you were. If it's meant for you to be that nice hundred and thirty-six pounds beautiful person, that you can be. Then why not start. If your happy with yourself then fine. I'm not suggesting that we all be clones, but it will be better for you. Yes, there will be people out there that will try and stop you. But, you can fight them, by using you control, (your will power.) Go all the way. Check with your family doctor. Tell Dr. White or Dr. Black that you will be starting a diet or weight loss program. He or she may have some suggestions in helping you. Listen to what they say by all means.

If by chance you don't like the weight loss programs that they put you on, then just cut down in what you're eating. Yes, it's hard to do that too, but it has to be done. Will you? Then go for a walk, even if it is only one block from your home and back, that is a great movement on your part. Get some friends together and have your own Walk Marathon. Each case is different, I know, but you have to get yourself on a Positive Note here. Think of what you could be doing if you didn't have that extra person off your back and relieving yourself of the Sixteen Tons that you have been carrying for so many years, You may think that it is hopeless and that you can't do it, but you can do it!!!

You may want to form a group in your neighborhood and call it, "Sixteen Tons And A Barrel Of Fun". Have your meetings once a week. Talk with each other. Tell your story so that the others will understand you and know where you're coming from. Anyone could be in the group. There is no discrimination in this group. Others who have done it could be there to support the family members or friends, and also the other members of the group. Then you could meet every morning or evening to go for a little walk. You also can walk both times. Then take it from there.

There is also group activities. When the group is on the same level go for a hike, even if it's around a park in town. Always start small, then graduate to the next level. And just keep on walking. You don't need to go to coast to coast. If you can, do other excursus to build whatever muscles to a certain point. To give them strength. Come and join the fight.

You don't want to be the way that you are for the rest of your life, do you? The answer is of course not. So lets do something about it then. Go for that walk, get a group together. Lets get on a Positive Note here. Say to yourself, "I can do it! I'll rake the challenge. I want to be a new me. I am tired of carrying this Sixteen Tons around with me. I don't want to be this person any more. I would like to change for the good. It's not because of what I see on the television or in the movies. Or what I may see in magazines. I don't want to keep up with the Jones's or Smith's. Just because Sue and April get certain things in life. The only think I would want out of like is love, A friendship kind of love. Whether it is from my family, friends that I know now, (to new friends that I will be meeting.) I would like to give it an old school try!! I can do it! I want to be lighter than I am now. It doesn't matter the sex at all. Men can do it too. Come on, guys. Woman can do the same thing to you. You don't have to Monopoly on it. What ever the problem we could do it back to you. Just because you've done it longer.

This writer is not telling you to give into society opinion. It is the fact, you'll feel a lot better. In every way, you'll feel this goodness about yourself. To rid of that twenty, fifty, a hundred, to two hundred pounds. Then maybe you could start on something else that you would like to do. Maybe take that trip to Europe, or to see Auntie Em or cousin Dave and could surprise them in what you have done. It may take six months for some, and two to three years for others, but at least it will be out of the way. You can see that grandchild become a doctor, lawyer, or anything that they want to become. Then you could be so proud of them and also of yourself.

What could I say to you out there in rural America or in those fine cities of ours. It may be time for you to move onto something else now and the weight would be in the way. Maybe there is something you'll be doing for the good. Think of all those good ideas that you have.

Do you want to be embarrassed at your own funeral? Either by eight men carrying you to your final resting place or they might have to use a crane to put you in your grave, as they would for a horse or elephant or other large animal. Unless you had decided to get yourself cremated. So you could lie next to your sweetheart or whoever.

What is it America? When are people going to start caring for others. To be nice to others. Everyone has feelings. I don't care who the hell you are in life, whether you're the President of some large corporation or a housekeeper for the rich and famous. There could be something that a heavy set person doesn't like about you. It doesn't matter how you're dressed. Or how much money you have in the bank here in America or in a Swiss Account. Some of you could be so ugly on the inside that you better think twice. With your thoughts and feelings on any subject. Think before saying anything. You talk about whoever comes into the same room that you're in. No wonder we are in bad shape. It's not only the United States, it's all over the world. When it this going to stop? Discrimination is a very ugly word. Think about it! You don't like this person, because of this and that. So what if someone is overweight. It's not what you look like, it's what inside the person. How come we have to hurt each other? Name calling might get you to do something that you'll regret for the rest of your life. Do you want that, do you?

Instead of ridiculing a person, because they are heavy. Why don't you get behind the scenes and wonder why this person is heavy. There are so many reasons why a person is, that the number goes off the scale. Sue and Harry can lose the ugly weight and you will still be the same old you, (a sour puss.) The ugly, they will always pick on something about the person that may enter their office, one day.

Here is a fine example of what could happen to one person in her life time. Of discrimination and lack of love and respect, plus understanding. We'll call her Alice. She was like any other child, so she thought. Happy go lucky and very content with what was going on with her life up until the age of ten. Then her world started to crumble. She was staying with her Aunt and Uncle for the summer, up on their farm in New York State. She looked and acted like any other child, but things were kept from her. Alice parents were getting a divorce. A nurse of all people, told Alice's mother that she was a Down Syndrome child and she would have to put her into Special Education. Her mother and grandfather found her at her aunt and uncles farm in New York State, and took her away from that safe heaven and took her somewhere when she didn't want to be. To Alice, the apartment building she was living in, looked like a prison. She thought that had done something wrong. It wasn't the apartment itself, it was just outside her window. When she looked out at it on this one Saturday morning, she had to look at this wall that had iron rods that had points at the end of them. In a sense they looked like arrows, but a little too big to put on a bow. For a year and a half, Alice was scared and afraid and didn't know what to make of it, and acted like it wasn't happening.

In May of nineteen sixty-two, both Alice and her mother were on a plane to Los Angeles. The four and a half hour trip was a memorable one. Alice felt happy. She loved to travel, even at the age of eleven and a half. A month short of her twelfth birthday. I guess even then, she knew that she would be doing a lot of traveling. It was in her blood and that she would be flying a lot in the years to come. Alice wasn't afraid of flying. It was good that she didn't, because it would take to long to get to where she might want to go. She may not have that much time or need to get from Los Angeles to New York in a hurry. Time will be to valuable to her in years to come.

Once in Los Angeles. Alice and her mother were like any other tourist for the ten days that they were in the area. They even saw some movie stars while they were going around the town. While going to a couple of the studios. She saw people like Jackie Cooper, Hugh O'Brian, and Robert Vaughan. She (Alice) felt comfortable in the studio and in the Los Angeles area, for some reason. The reason could be as simple as writing a simple story that would bring her to the top.

Was there something telling her that in the very near or far future that she would like in the Los Angeles area and work at a couple of the studios with some of the stars of the time. To get some of her stories on the mighty screen. Or, that she'll only live in the area and will be well known for what she will write, when the time comes. Will she be famous as that feeling was trying to tell her, as she didn't know what it had meant at the time. What did it mean for Alice, I wonder.

When they settled in their new apartment. They had this nice Italian couple as landlords, in the city of Monterey, California. Still unaware that she was in Special Education, and what was really happening behind the scenes. A lot of thing were kept from her. The mother and whoever knew this information, thought it was best that she didn't know. Well, it wasn't, at least in her opinion.

When she did get the nerve to write to her and written the return address on the envelope, she wished that she hadn't, because when Alice received a letter from her, it stated that her grandfather had died about a month later, after she left the area. It was due to cancer. Alice went into some kind of shock. She couldn't believe it. It was something that she had no control over. It was the first man that she really loved and respected and just wondered why he was taken from her. A lot of things went through her mind. The tears started to come, and when they did, they came in buckets. She was angry, confused and wanted her grandfather back and wanted his love and support. That's highly unlikely that he could come back. This is when she went into a shell and built a wall between her and the outside world. It was something to see, all right.

This is where it all started for Alice. Without knowing it, she started watching movies, even though she may have seen the movie before. From such movies as, "Hamlet" "Othello" to "Spartacus" to something like "The Sound Of Music" to "Mary Poppins" to any of the Disney movies. Just to get her in some fantasy world of her own and not believing that the world is like the way it is.

Of course, when the weight went on, the names and the discrimination had started. She didn't care, what other people thought of her, because they were not true friends or that were just bullies and or wanted to be a wise guy, and thought they knew best. Of course, the remarks that they said to Alice put her into more of a shell. Some of the remarks hurt her and didn't help the situation, but as the years went by, Alice just let it ride. That people like that will get their day. The bullies and the people that like to discrimination against a person that do have a weight problem, will have their day. Just because they didn't give her or John Do a job or called them a Miss Piggy or other names.

Alice can deal with her problem by losing the weight. America and other place in the world will still have their problems of the ugly word called discrimination. That is worse than the weight problem or any other problem that a person may have. If we could get rid of that and help them, this world would be a lot better. One person could be a crusader. Sure, they could start something, but it takes time and money also. Some times you would need a sponsor. It would take a very long time to build up a friendship between two people, that have the same problem. They would have to change the person a price for their traveling time and their advice, somewhat like a counselor. With most people living on a limited income or a low income they couldn't do something like this or go to Jenny Craig or to Weight Watchers or any other program out there.

As for someone like myself or for someone like Alice. We are people that have reached to a certain level of being a tough person, (in a manner of speaking.) It doesn't bother us any more and we could live like this for the rest of our lives, if we had too.

We have the right stuff to be that counselor or that certain person that could listen. And give you that Positive Note that you may need or that you may want. But if we do not have a meeting place to meet, then, I do not know what I could say. Or even with the car, or should I say with the van that I have will fall apart at any moment. Even if I went to the great city of Fullerton to Newport Beach to see you in your home or apartment.

Alice and I are here to give you this boost and think about what was said here in this story and that you could start doing it on your own. Take your time. It all will take time. Especially the one's that are extremely overweight. You didn't put it on overnight, though it may of have felt like it. You can't take it off overnight. Rome wasn't built in a day, either.

Maybe this will help you get to the starting line and start to do something, like cutting down your intake a little or going for that walk, but get moving.

[This is Rose and Kim at Universal Studios, in Hollywood. A day that they will never forget as long as they live.]

Chapter Seven
The Gift

Imagine if you were in this person's shoes. What would do you, if one of your friends came to you and asked you if you would like to go with them on a trip to California and your expenses would be paid for? Would you think that this person was joking or would you think to yourself, "What did I do to deserve this? Maybe, it was a gift from Jesus for a number of reasons or maybe just for one This is what I (Sara) think is what happened to Kim.

Still after several months after she took the trip, she was still on that amazement cloud and really didn't expect something like that would happen to her. The fact is that we did so much in one week and then other places have a lot to do. I'm just wondering if people think of what? Some times I don't know about some people. I know they are smart people out there, but they simply just don't think at all. What gives? When Kim wrote to me in some of her letters, that she still thinks about it every now and again, which is fine to do. I given her some new ideas to think about, but I knew I would still have to go and tell her a few things and my side of the story, maybe that would help her understand this whole thing. There was something that Kim was missing.

A few days later, I arrived at my aunt Rose's home. Everyone there was surprised to see me. I was so happy to be there for a couple of reasons. One was to check on my youngest cousin, and to meet other members of the family that I haven't met as yet or haven't seen since they were in diapers. Doing a lot of things while I was there, instead of just going to see Kim. Arriving at seven o'clock in the evening on a Tuesdays night. I asked Rose if she would call Kim and set up for the following night. Rose remarked that it would be their prayer meeting night and she would be there, but called to double checked. I asked her if she would leave it as a surprise where I was concerned for a couple of reasons. One was to talk with a man of the cloth, anyway. To give us some answers that I could get from all directions and for Kim to look at it from my stand point. To maybe opening up her eyes and mind. Kim answers maybe in what I was going to tell her and the others. I knew that I couldn't wait. There was going to be a lot to talk about. But first, I was going to tell her my side of the story. Plus the few ideas I came up with. I asked Rose that I would like the minister there, so he could answer a couple of the questions that might come up.

Everyone sat down and I asked them to listen to my side of this whole thing, and it wouldn't take long. Or some of my ideas of why Kim came along. It was really an eye opener and to wake her up to the fact that she could see anything that she wanted to see, if she wanted too. Sure, there is time for fun and a time where you have to have a daily routine of this and that.

It all started on December 24, 1989, when I called my aunt Rose to wish her a Merry Christmas and to see what was going on. Much to my surprise I received a Christmas present by phone. I didn't realize it until afterwards. It was the fact that she told me that her and her two daughters were planning to come out to California sometime soon. Rose was going to find some way of getting out there and see what it was all about after all these years. I've been telling her things about this state. When Rose said that and a few other things, like, "Even if I have to beg, borrow, or steel it". I knew that she was coming out all right. After the shock and the amazement wore off. I started to think of all the different places I could take them. I didn't know where to begin. I still needed a few questions answered, but I knew I would get the answers sooner or later. I wasn't going to be concerned about it for awhile.

By this time, a few months had pasted and still no word. Since Rose isn't much of a writer and neither were my two cousins that were to come with her. This one night I was sitting on the sofa and started to think about them. I knew I was going to take them to Disneyland, Universal Studios, but before I could think of another thing, the phone rang. It turned out to be Rose with her million questions of when is the best time to come out there and which is the best airlines and the other questions that goes with that line of questioning. She knew I had a lot of traveling experience. I gave her the answers she needed. I asked her a few questions and they were answered. Everyone was happy, for the time being.

The time was flying by as usual. Another three months went by once again and still no word and if they were coming out at the end of June, which was three weeks away. I wanted some answers. It was eating at me for some reason, not only that I had to make the last minute plans and see if my calendar was free for the week or whatever length of time they were here. This time I called Rose and asked her the million and one questions. Her answers were that it wouldn't be until the twenty ninth of August to September Fifth. It was the best that she could do and that she had to get touch with Diana to see what her story was in regarding to the trip at hand.

Now, I have something to work with. I didn't know there was going to be so much work into this. I started to really pray. That all of them could come. I guess that prayer wasn't going to be answered, because a couple of weeks later, I received my birthday card from Rose. It stated that Diana and Katie (the two daughters) will not be coming for different reasons and that she was bringing a girlfriend. You know how you would feel when you get some news and it's not to good or you might be a little disappointed, because you wanted it to be another way or at least see one of your cousins, in my point of view. Hope for the best and that the next time they will come with or without their mother. "What can you do?" The answer would be nothing.

Life is full of surprises all right. It's the unknown that really gets us. The unexpected of that period of time will go. Of how people can disappoint you by backing out of something.

I didn't realize it then, but that God had his own version or reasons for this, so he could show Kim that there is more to life then what she was doing before the big question from Rose. Sure, to serve him, but to have a life and to enjoy it and to have something to look forward too, for the future. Not just doing the same thing day in and day out and so forth down the line. To do other things and to go out there and see what other places have to offer. Even just to visit and see their new friends and doing something.

At this time I written to Rose. I wanted the flight information. There were a few reasons. One is, of course to meet them at the airport. Two, is to know what time the flight was coming and all that. Three is because I just wanted it for my own satisfaction. I didn't want anything to happen that day by all means. I was thinking and talking with God and thanking Him for everything, so far. I didn't want anything to happen before I left for the airport. I knew I had to think positively from now on. Ever since I received the flight information on their arrival. The vibrations from the envelope and the sheet of paper that the information was on. It was telling me something was going to happen, beside the information that was on there. Not know whether it was good or bad, but there was something there and it wasn't too good. As each day, and each minute that went by got a little closer to the big day. I couldn't help the way I felt about this whole thing. That's the way it was. I knew that I couldn't help the way I was feeling. I knew Rose would call if there was any bad news or if she wasn't coming, but every time the phone rang, I jumped five feet off of the ground and hoped that it wasn't her or one of the family members saying that she wasn't coming for whatever reason. I was so nervous those last two weeks, it wasn't even funny. Time will only tell. Life is strange sometimes.

I was so glad I had all the diversions that I did have. I know it helped quite a bit. With a friend of mine by the name of Charlie coming into town for a visit and we only seen each other for an hour or so. He wasn't going to be in town for very long. I just wished he had called me back so we could get together and done something, but no such luck. Then the agency I some times work for, called me. I was glad that I told then what I was going to do and from the twenty ninth of August to September fifth. I was going to be late. Knowing how things came in bushes, it did for me this time. It always happens.

D-DAY was finally here. There was no turning back now. Everything was arranged there was no more to do. I asked Allen (a friend of mine) to take me to the airport. I didn't think that I could of driven myself or have take the airport bus, because of the time involved. We left about ten. So that we would have plenty of time to get there and not knowing the traffic situation was like on the ninety-one and the other freeways to get there. We had plenty of time to spare. I didn't even say two words to Allen on the way up. After getting out of the car and started walking in the wrong direction. I said to him, "Aren't we going the wrong way? Because I felt that it was in the other way. I didn't know where he figured it would be in a different building. We started going the other way. He may of thought they were all departures. And that we had go to another terminal for the flights that were coming in. Well, I wanted to check in that terminal that was over there. I didn't want to miss

77

anything and thank good that we had plenty of time. This was to important for me to be ending up somewhere else. And to waste the time at the wrong place. Have you ever felt that everything come all at once. Then you have nothing to do for some time. This is the way that I felt those last two weeks. I just wished I could do this all the time, being busy doing whatever. It worked out for the best anyway of talking or seeing the four people that come out of town wanting to see me.

After Allen and I checked the monitor for the flight number to see what gate and if the plane was coming in on time. I was so glad that it was and I couldn't wait for that half an hour to go by as it was. I didn't know that how I made it through. It felt like we were waiting thirty hours instead of thirty minutes. At the gate we sat down and waited and watched the other people coming and wishing that it was all over. I thought I was waiting for someone to have a baby, because it was nine months since that new beginning or from the start of this whole thing, and this baby was four and a half days over due. (Just Stubborn,) and (it was twenty-one years old.) Time was going to slow for me. I wished that it was time to hug my aunt and to meet Kim, (the friend that was coming with her.) What a day this turned out to be.

Since I knew what it was like to travel. I knew what level they were at. They only had eight minutes to touch down. I was higher than a kite in that nice blue sky. Up in the clouds about the whole thing. I walked back and forth, like waiting for someone to come and say some thing or something to have a baby, like I said before. The excitement was getting too much. The plane landed and was taxing to the terminal. I wondered if that was the plane, seeing so many before, passing by and if they were on it and hoped that they weren't the last ones out of there. Some times people will wait till the right time or when it's less crowded before leaving the vehicle of any kind. The moment of truth will come. They opened the double doors. I was standing behind the roped area and really didn't have a clear view of the area they were walking out of, but much to my surprise they weren't too far in the middle of all this. I caught a glimpse of my aunts face since I didn't know what Kim looked like. I got her attention and said hello and all that. She walked around the pillar to get on the right side and introduce Kim. We walked over to pickup Allen on the way to pickup their bags. To getting all the introductions out of the way. The room was filled with excitement, from all directions. I thought everyone was going to explode there for awhile, this was something to see, by all means.

On the way to the car, the girls wanted a picture of themselves when they first arrived here in Los Angeles. We all stood right in the middle of one of the driveways. In the background was some palm trees so that they could show off. I could hear them already with the rest of the people they told it too. Saying it over and over again. I was so glad that one of these crazy drivers didn't come right then and there and tired and start something.

Once we got onto the 405 freeway, they were amazed at what they were seeing and the questions that they were asking and the different kinds of palm trees and the other kinds of plants that we had out here. I was so happy, I knew that they would be needing the attention and full of questions and comments. I knew I couldn't of done it alone. I could of, but didn't.

Once at the apartment, we took the suitcases out of the trunk and started to go upstairs. Rose asked Allen why he wasn't coming with us. He told her, he had to go back to work. I gave the girls the directions of going through the front gate and then making a left and start going up the stairs. I couldn't help but to say, "We're Here!!! (Stretching the word here.) My mother couldn't believe her eyes, when she had seen my aunts gray hair, and even remarked about it. She may of thought that I may of picked up the wrong people. How could she have thought that?

The day of joyous for all of us. We all were so happy. After getting my aunt out here after twenty years of writing to her and telling her all the things that I did. After putting their bags into my room and they both got out a little gift for both of us, which wasn't expected.

The afternoon was full with all kinds of news, (good and bad.) Of my cousins Katie terrible car accident to the nice visit that my aunt had with my brother Harry. As I was listening to them talking. Now I get some of the answers to those feelings that I felt.

Then the phone rang. This time it was Tommy, he didn't know what to do with himself and there was something that he had to show me, it could of waited till after my aunt and Kim went home. I had to excuse myself for about a half an hour or so. I quickly took care of seeing the broken glass at this friends of mine place, someone had ran into the place with their truck or car. I hoped that he would not bother me until Rose and Kim were gone, knowing that boy, he won't. He needs some help, badly.

On the want back to the apartment. I thought to myself, "Boy, the girls are in for a big treat this week!" At least I knew the majority of the places that we were going to. They were going to wish they could stay. But at this point in time, my mother and I didn't know what it would be like at where we were going this evening, (Medieval Times.) Or how well the show was going to be, expect what we did hear from others that had already gone to the show. You really get involved with the show and think that you're really back in that period of time with King Arthur. By the time I got home, the girls were in my bedroom supposedly taking a nap, but I knew they were too excited and all that. With it being their first trip and anytime that anyone takes a vacation, no matter where a person goes. A person wants to go somewhere at least for a couple of hours or so on the first day anyhow, especially if a person gets a few extra hours.

The evening came and it went and so did the rest of the week. It came as fast as it went. We'll never forget it for the rest of our lives. We all were still in the dark about a lot of things, but were cleared up as the week went on. Of why I was so nervous those two weeks before and getting to know Kim, since my mother (Nora) and I just met her. We had all enjoyed ourselves that night with the rest of the audience.

After we had stopped at one of the stores to pickup a few things and went home and went to bed. I had forgotten all about the fireworks from Disneyland on at nine-thirty and being their first night. Sometimes they can be so loud that they might of thought there might have been a shooting in the neighborhood. I went out there to check to see if they might have been awaken by this, but when I got there, they were asleep like babies. Though the next morning, Kim said that she heard them, but didn't bother about getting up, because of her time clock inside her body had said that it was twelve thirty, when it was actually it was nine-thirty. Their bodies had to get use to the different time zones. I would be doing the same thing if I was in their shoes. Besides they could see the fireworks anytime that they were here. I guess they were really loud that night was because of the fact that it was do to my aunt Rose being here. A big celebration for everyone. (Even if it was all in my mind that it was just for Rose being here after twenty years of telling her.

From this point on was a green light, because from that point on we were on the go, from the tour of Universal Studios the next day and the on Friday was Movie land Wax Museum and the Dancing Waters that night, to Disneyland on Saturday. Sunday was two churches, plus a movie.

Monday was the beach and on Tuesday was a day to pack and do anything that was left out. The topping on the cake was the Crystal Cathedral for the both of them. With something like that to go through whether it's was your first time or your hundredth time to California. It was out of this world for Rose and Kim. With every passing day was a new experience for the both of them. But by doing something like this or maybe not expecting some thing like this, I don't know what they thought they were going to do once they had got here, but I knew for one thing that I wasn't going to do was just sit there and do nothing. With all the places that are out here and do anything. It would be foolish not to take them to the best places first.

I thought to myself before and even while they were here that I would have more time with my aunt, because there was something that I wanted to talk to her about, but never got it off the ground. I knew that if there was more time then I could of, but there wasn't. With only having a week and doing all those things that we did, it's a miracle in itself. I knew everything could happen in that week. It was time for Kim to open up and see what it was like out in the world and to have this time for learning and to take it from there, that is what a person could do.

The day that they left was the worse day that I experienced. It felt like the bus had some kind of hook or hanger or something hooked to the bumper and just taken my inner soul. I knew that I was going to cry a little, but not to the point to where it was raining the way that it was. I had made myself sick or that you might think something was being taken out of my body without any kind of medicine. Rose cried too, but not as bad as I was. We all enjoyed the week so much that I guess we wanted some more. In reality we didn't get any. I knew there would be a next time. Things had to get back to normal and back to work and other things will always be there. The first time in a long time I felt goo about the whole thing and to go back to the dull life that I had at the time was something else, even in the land of plenty.

Now this is the part where I think that Kim is still in that stage of learning with her writing letters and with her asked all kinds of questions, like did it take long to plan something like that and to her surprise that I had written a book. I finished it before they came, but there was a few things to do with it and not only that work after they left to back to their lives in their little town or cities. There was one thing I wanted to add their chapter of the week of being here with the other information that is in there. Let alone retyping the whole thing over again of three hundred and eighty pages of this thing. Not an easy thing to do. Even then I wouldn't know if I could get the thing published somewhere on my own or through an agent. Agents are some times harder to get then the publishers.

When I started to really think about this was when I received a letter from Kim in May of the following year. I started from the beginning just like I did just now so that everyone could get the whole picture. And how everyone was so much in the dark about it, as I mentioned before. Things could have been a lot different than they were. Of maybe the fact my mother calling Rose and telling her not to bring this woman with her for whatever reason or reasons and how could we ask her for her share of the expenses and any other questions that my mother would of come with, but it didn't happen. This is when I got the idea that Kim had gotten "The Gift" from Jesus. It started with my aunt paying for the airlines and the rest my mother and I paid for. Where else would you get a gift like that, that's what I would like to know? Of two strangers doing something like that. So that she could learn and take it from there, but if she didn't she would miss a lot of things.

Maxwell, (the minister) agreed with me up to a point that it was a Gift from Jesus and that she should use the data that she received. He wanted to know where I had got this information. I simply told him that what other explanation was there. I might not have an I.Q. of a hundred and eighty, but I can sure figure that one out, because I was one of Gods children that have her something to last for the rest of her life, let alone my aunt.

There is a lesson in there for Kim, if she really looks for it. Sure to do the daily routine and go to church and anything else that may of happen in your daily life. But when you save your money and go out there and see the different places that you would like to see. It's a class room out there. Even if it takes you a couple of years to save for it, whether it's to California or anywhere else. Whether you do it with a friend or relative or just go out there and see for yourself. Have something to look forward too.

Everyone was taking all this information quite well. I thought that there might be a little bit of something there. Everyone wanted to wait till I finished with what I was saying before saying anything themselves.

There is another point that I would like to bring up. That maybe someday you could do the same thing for Rose and treat her in coming to California or where you are planning to go. Just don't say something like you would like to go here and there and don't do nothing about it. Don't think "Gifts" like that come around every year or every six months or so. As far as I'm concerned that you don't have to do anything for me. The fun and enjoyment was my pleasure was all mine on my part, but on the other hand, my mother might think differently. She doesn't say it then, but when she does, watch out. I think at this time, she will let it ride. If there is a next time. There will be a little change, anybody or everyone that comes will have to pay for their own share of what goes on during the time that they are out there. If you figure it out for the three of us, (Rose, Kim and I,) it cost a hundred and thirty dollars a person to get into the places that we did. Let alone for meals and for transportation. Let alone the places that my mother went with us and all the other things.

Some people are quite lucky and should be thanking Jesus for what they had received, which they did. Then there is something else that just came to me, supposing Diane and Katie did say yes to their mother and went with her. Then the only thing Kim would be hearing it second hand instead of first hand or if it happened the both said yes and that Katie still went through the terrible accident. Do you expect Rose to think of you at a time like that? Maybe Katie would have to pay for her own ticket. Then Rose would have to give Katie the three hundred dollars or whatever back to Katie. How would you know if Rose would of asked you or simply went back to her son Bert and told him to get the money back or put someone else's name on the ticket. Sure there are reasons for all this, but I think Jesus had a lot to do with it. We all have our daily lives, but also have some fun and the excitement like what we had. Just don't read it out of a Mystery novel or any other kinds of books, go and see the places you want to see some of the old ones. Put some spark and excitement into your life. I know what it's like to come fro ma small town or city is something and then go into something like Los Angeles must have been a bid surprising or a big move on your part. I know I have done it myself. In many ways I have experienced the same things as you and Kim. That's why the week was the way it was.

My last point that I want to get across for everyone, is to know this. Supposing that you had taken the same trip, but there would be a big difference and that is the both of you would be staying at a motel or hotel somewhere and there wouldn't be no Sara or Norma. You wouldn't of seen half of the things you did see or went to the places that you might not like as much as you did. There wouldn't be no plan of any kind and would have to ask someone that maybe one of the employees of the motel where you are staying at upon which is the best places to see and they might not be the best in your eyes. I know for sure that you girls would of done a lot of shopping and maybe not even at Mickey's Corner. I know that you wouldn't of done all those things, because it was all planned out and we went to a number of the best places. All the places here is Southern California are the best, but that's if you like those places and with only having a week, you can't go everywhere. I really thought about this whole thing and that's the way that it came out. I know what you and Rose were going through. Because I went through the same thing as you did, (in nineteen sixty-two.) All I can say now is you have something to look forward to and I hope you'll use it.

Kim and the others were overwhelmed by the things I told them. There was silence after I told them all this. Total amazement. I was surprised that Maxwell didn't start it up right away, but Rose had to put her two cents into it by saying, "Why didn't you say something before this? I would of come alone, if you asked me. As for the "Gift" from Jesus, where did that come from? I told them, "It's the only answer that I could come up with, because you needed someone with you, aunt Rose. To get you over the hump dealing with Katie. It was meant for Kim to come. Maxwell stepped in and said that he agreed with me and that it was the only explanation it could have been.

On the other hand, Kim needed to think about it. It was to much for her to comprehend all at once. Sure think about it, but don't think about it too long. As the world will go by as fast as it comes and you won't see a thing or do a thing. It was the only way that Kim could do anything if she wanted what she wanted out of life. Is to just save and do without whatever it is to get something more delightful and more memorable to her and to give her the ideas of where to go if she wanted to relocate somewhere. It may not be California, but it might be somewhere else. You never know what the LORD Jesus has in store for you, whether it is California or some other place. Each start has it's own little something. Either with snow and ice or earthquakes or they might not have as much as other places or you like what they might have in that state. It might have what your looking for.

In closing: It's not only Kim and the others, it's any of you out there that could be in the same situation like this. It maybe a little different, but whatever you do, go out there and do what is meant for you. Your dreams or ideas will just be that if they don't do something about it, because I (Sara) have gotten an inspiration like that I wouldn't waste any time about it. I would be starting right now or soon afterwards of getting something started or doing something about it. I wouldn't be sitting in a rocking chair or any kind of chair and wished that I had thought of it first.

CHAPTER EIGHT
"THIS ONE IS FOR YOU, GRANDPA!!

Have you ever lost a loved one and you loved them so much that it felt like someone was pulling your heart out with a anchor. The pain is so great that it tops the scales. Your mind is confused and wants to be protected by all things possible. Twelve is not an easy age to take some information like that, especially when you're a sensitive child and love this man who was your grandfather for only nine years of your life. Still wanting some more time with. To asking him to come back, when it was highly impossible.

Imagine if you were this child. How would you like to have a bomb shell put on you. Never in a million years thinking that it wouldn't ever happen to you. Here you are at the age of ten and in total darkness about mostly everything. Though acting like any ten year old, because what you don't know won't hurt you. In many ways it does hurt you when it comes to your attention.

New York State, 1959. I (Cathy) was staying with my aunt and her family for a brief time. I thought I was on top of the world. Enjoying myself with my cousins, including an afternoon walk with nature. It may have been only five miles, but you tell your aunt that you went five hundred miles, because it was so long and finding all sorts of things on the way. Of bones from a bull or a cow to any other large animal. To all the different bushes and trees that we saw. To me, I felt like I was living a experience of a LITTLE HOUSE ON THE PRAIRIE. I loved being there. There was a shadow that was coming very soon. One of the first hurts of my life.

This one Saturday afternoon, Katie and I were up in our room playing a game of cards. We heard some voices arguing downstairs. Katie heard it first. WE wondered what was going on down there. I tried to hear what was going on, but it was a little hard to understand, because they were going a little to fast. My mother and her father came to the house to get me. They sounded like they were really at it. Of why a mother shouldn't have her own daughter and why she shouldn't be with her, but on the other side of the coin, my aunt told her, that she shouldn't be taken away like this and that her brother had the right to put his daughter anywhere he wanted to and that was a loving family and with other children.

With whatever else was talked about in this fifteen minutes time spanned. At the end of that period, my aunt came to the bottom of the stairs and called out my name. Jessica (my aunt) told me a few things and to go upstairs and get my stuff and that I would be going with my mother and other grandfather. I replied by saying, "OK, I will." "Cathy, there is no need for that. You will come with me." said the mother. I think what it was, is that my mother didn't trust that something else wouldn't happen and somehow would kidnap me and hide me somewhere else on the property or some other crazy idea she may have had in her head.

As we were walking to the car, I was totally in the dark. I didn't know what was going on. I didn't know there was a ugly divorce battle. Nor any of the other stuff. The major thing that was going to happen was. In a very short time, my grandfather was going to die and would leave me and to be on my own from then on.

To this day, I can see myself looking out the back window of the car waving to them. I felt torn and want to be with them. The hurt was there, but it wasn't as bad as what was going to be coming up. Maybe that is why some things have come about in my life that bother me today. The answer to the question is, that it has to do with relationships, maybe that's why I don't have many friends or don't want to get close to anyone. No matter if they are a man or a woman.

With the year and a half in Maryland was like hell. We lived in this apartment that was surrounded by a brick wall with some kind of iron spokes pointing up. If felt like a prison. It looked like in from the inside out. The apartment was great, but not look outsold. I was glad went we were on the plane to Los Angeles.

For the next ten days or so. My mother and I went to the different places around Southern California. Like any tourist, we saw everything. In this part, I was happy and delighted. I didn't have a carry in the world. I didn't have a clue that in a month to six weeks I would be getting a letter from my aunt Jessica stating some facts that I wouldn't like at all.

After moving into this nice apartment unit in a different city as lively as Monterey, California. Adjusting quite well. I've always loved to see movies and been drawn to some of them more than others. Like to "Spartacus", "Hamlet", "My Fair Lady", "The Sound of Music", all different types of stories. I guess I was surprising my feelings, because I didn't know what was going on and being in a new town or city. It could be the fact that I was starting a new hobby. It wasn't easy being in the dark. Though I was acting like any other child and not being rebels or anything of that nature. It didn't come to me until much later in life of why I like "Spartacus". Like he did in the movie was to be free. I felt trapped and lost and needed something to make me set free.

By this time, I all ready sent a letter to my aunt. I was trying to break through some of the walls of fear that was in me. My thoughts were going all over the place at the time I wrote the letter. I know it was the fear I had inside me, of what my mother's reaction would be. Though in the back of my mind I knew the distance was great and didn't have any fear of them coming to get me or try to rescue me. I like it where I was at. Traveling turns out to be one of my favorite things to do. When it was time for me to go wherever. Though I didn't know what was going to happen when I received the letter from my aunt. This was the tragedy of all times. I didn't know what she was going to write back to me. The pen is sharper then the mighty sword.

Within the week, I received the letter. I quickly opened it. I was so happy for the moment, because I gotten the letter and there was someone else in my life once again. I was lying down on my bed while I was reading this. I couldn't believe what it was saying. I read it over and over again. I know I went into some kind of shock, but after it wear off, I went into some kind of heet. This was after I shown the letter to my mother. I just took the letter back and took the doll I had and went back into the bedroom. The answer that my mother gave me wasn't satisfactory.

I even told to the LORD and asked HIM, WHY? Of course I didn't get an answer then, so I thought. The tears were coming down so fast that I could of made the pacific ocean all over again. This is what I thought at the time. I also said to the LORD a lot of other things. In time I got all those answers. I didn't help me at that time, I thought I was going through hell and on the verge of some mental break down. The torture I was going through was behind words to express it. This is when I built a wall around myself. I never wanted to be hurt ever again. By going to the movies and seeing, "SPARTACUS", "HAMLET", over and over again. With one wanting the freedom like, "SPARTACUS" and the tragedy of "HAMLET". This is what I was in. So I just stayed behind that wall for quite sometime. Though I did feel this presents with me, but it wasn't my grandfather, it was more of a woman's presents. I didn't give her a name or did she tell me then. Bonnie, (the woman was an angel.) Her main job was to comfort, counsel, a companion. She has turn out to be a great friend through out the years. Someone like a sister, cousin, a person I could talk with. Besides the LORD Jesus, or the HOLY FATHER, OR HOLY SPIRIT. Bonnie was a comfort zone and also the sister that I never had. If she didn't come or wasn't sent into my life, I wouldn't know where I would have been right now.

Maybe that's why I maybe having trouble with my relationships. With the divorce and the lose of my grandfather (mostly.) Plus having a brother that is cold as a piece of ice, because of the way he felt. Of not getting enough love from our mother and whatever other reasons he may have. There was a lot jealousy and rebel the way he did. No wonder he is on his third wife and still so one sided. He doesn't want to let his fears go, either.

This maybe the cause of why I don't have that many friends, especially in dealing with a man or a more serious role. It seems it was the wrong situation. I knew I wasn't experienced enough, in dealing with men or woman. I know I wasn't experienced enough, but I didn't need to have a man that was married, on drugs or alcohol, or just wanted a one night stand. I didn't want to close to anyone, being afraid of losing them, also or be being hurt in some way.

So how could a person get onto the right road and to not be afraid of getting hurt and not have the wrong kind of people in their lives. To meeting someone who is sweet and kind and who doesn't have a problem with drugs alcohol or who want to be controlling, demanding and self-centered and who wants someone to be their salve, so that he could be a master over this people. That is not for me, nor it shouldn't be for anyone else.

So what can a person do in this kind of situation? What would you do if you were in Cathy's shoes? This question could be for anyone. It could of happened to either side of the coin.

Think of this story. There are so many people that have been a child of divorce and have lost a grandparent at a very young age, (and loved that grandparent so much that they thought they were going mad.) But somehow came out of the madness. A child who didn't ask for this. Nor this woman wants to go through this any more. So where could a person go? Where else but to the LORD, but he hasn't yet answered. So that Cathy could get over this mountain and to deal with other things, so she could deal with other mountains, she has in her life.

Oh no wonder I am only at the stage where I am at. First of all, being at the end of the pay scale, not getting more work them I should be getting. For not going back to school and taking something that would get me a better position in life. To being expected in more places. To having the doors open more freely, instead of being that joker or class clown so that other people could laugh. It feels like their laugh at me, instead of with me. I don't mind being the clown, as long as they are laughing with me, but I do need to move on.

When will it be my turn for something better than this?

When will God see that I am honest about my prayers, no matter if they as for myself or for someone else. I want my soul to waken to what I am suppose to be doing. My heart is reaching out and it is honest as it can be. I like doing other things for other people, no matter how small or big. I just don't feel as important as I should be. When will it be my turn?

IN THE NAME OF JESUS, HELP ME!!

CHAPTER NINE
"TO LOOK WITHIN YOURSELF!!

Discrimination in this country is way to out of hand, that it could fill the Atlantic and the Pacific Oceans. With all the kinds of discrimination you can think of. The most discriminated person is the one that is overweight. Weather it is from a family member to a complete stranger. It doesn't help any with whatever your doing to the person at hand. You maybe using reverse psychology, but as you can see, it is not working. It maybe out of love, but try some thing else. This maybe a suggestion, by taking Jack or Heather with you to the place where your going. Have them join in, in whatever it is. They may want to start slowly in some kind of exercise program, to build their confidence. Then, building from there. Before you know it, the weight will be coming off. As long as they are cutting down on their food also.

With most of us being to ashamed to be with a fat or overweight person, because of the reason you may have in your mind. When they could be the greatest person, you'll ever know. He or she could be the person your looking for. Whatever the need you may have for a person like them. It could be for anything. Just don't give them the job and they will only be stuffing envelopes to answering the phones. Yes, a person has to start at the bottom of the totem pole in the company, but gee whiz, give a person a break. This person could turn out to be your best friend after awhile. America, get to know us. We did not come from outer space, nor did the weight get on there over night. No matter how the weight got there, it could be easily taken off, but you will still have this thing about overweight people. Change it for the good.

Now that we're so proud America and would fight to keep terrorist from what they might do. What about a different kind of terrorism. That could hurt a persons spirit, a persons self-worth, their confidence, and their worth in life. It doesn't help to name calling, to nag them to start to lose the weight or wonder how all the weight got there. Everyone has their beginnings of how they started with just using food as a friend, a companion, to a comfort, to anything else they may call it. People are only looking on the outside. What happens if you look beyond the fat and the ugliness, you would find a whole different person that could be the right kind of person to be that friend, to working for you in some way, (even if it's behind the scene on a temporary basics, till they lose the sixty, eight, a hundred or two hundred pounds.) It is up to the person to start their own program, with the help of a doctor, (to make sure they get whatever physical.) Even if its to cut back on those many hamburgers, donuts, to whatever chose of food. To cut it back by one, then let sometime go by and cut anything one back. To where you could get to the point of having one every once in awhile or none at all. It is all in the training of your mind. Listen Rome wasn't built in a day, nor did the weight get there over night. Time can be on your side, if you let it. Be honest with yourself, you do not to be like this for the rest of your life, unless you on a level of being comfortable with whatever weight you are. That's fine, but someday, you will consider losing whatever weight. You would feel a lot better and maybe have a dream come true, if we didn't weigh _____ pounds. It's up to you.

As things started to unveil in my life. I (Cathy) had an over protective mother, for one thing and gave me any food that I wanted, weather it was right or wrong. I guess with my mother's up bringing with her father was something out of this world, with the type of man he was. When my brother and I came along, things were a lot different. Not just some kind of candy bar to a lot of the wrong things a person should eat all the time.

The weight didn't start appearing until I was twelve or thirteen years old. With being totally in the dark about what was going on. No one considers the children. They might think they are, pending on the situation. I'm just glad that people are getting out of those drama scenes, for a better situations. Instead of living in a hell type form mate.

Imagine this, living in New York State with your aunt and uncle, plus your six cousins. The ages from the age of twelve to a ten month old. At this time, I didn't know that my aunt had or was going to have a miscarriage or else I wouldn't have seven cousins. Though almost fifty two years ago when my aunt as with my cousin Judy and didn't know that she could have been having another child again, and this time, she was suppose to have a set of twins, because she was still having her period and in the process Jessica lost one of the children. (It turned out to be another boy.) With six boys and two girls would have been something else. I wished I could have been in that family. I am, but as a cousin. Things did turn out will. It wasn't until fifty-one years later, (through DNA), this is when the news was found out.

As in everyday life with chores, church, and everything else. To me seemed like a normal things of every day life. This one afternoon, the five of us went for a walk. It turned out to be a nature walk with all the different flowers, bushes, and bones from a very large animal, (a cow, a bull or a horse.) The time it took us, in which didn't seem that long, (two to two and a half hours.) Quality time well spend. It was awful nice to have the time with them in the setting that it was. Something I'll always remember for the rest of my days.

Of course at the age of nine, I wasn't expecting the unexpected. I was till in the dark about a lot of things, especially in the case of the divorce and separation of my parents. I was just an innocent by standard. It may of not looked like it, but it was there. I felt like I was going for the ride and it was some ride all right.

At this time, my mother and her father were in the living room, arguing with my aunt and uncle about who should be the care provider of me. I didn't know that my mother didn't know where this place was and this force or energy was guiding her to the house. I don't even remember how I got there, because I think I have blocked out the first twelve years of my life. All because of the news I received two years later.) Judy and I were upstairs in our room, when we heard all this commotion going on and I asked Judy, "Do you hear that. I wonder what's going on? Do you have any ideas." Her respond was, "I don't know! Your guess is good has mine!"

All of this was going on for at least a good twenty minutes, before my aunt called out to me and asked if I would come downstairs. Judy stood at the top of the stairs, just passed where the stairs stopped turning. While I went to see what her mother wanted. Jessica spoke to me softly and said that I would have to go with my mother and other grandfather. I didn't want to. I didn't like that grandfather, because of a few things he had done. Child Abuse and being cruel to an animal, (by putting a dog asleep for no reason whatsoever.) (I can still feel him kicking me in the ribs.) I was doing nothing wrong and minding my own business. By watching TV and had a few toys on the floor. (He was a neat freak.) Well when there are children around, there is going to be toys and there going to be around, until the child puts in its rightful place.

I remembered getting into my grandfathers car. I was facing to the back window. I was standing on my knees.

Everyone was standing on the dirt road. My heart was crying as I was waving good-bye and not knowing if I would ever see them again. I waved until I couldn't see them no more. The pain was sharp, like a knife going right through you. This is how bad it had gotten, though it didn't show at all. I stayed on the same level as I was, but in a different way. No one knew that I had changed somewhat.

I may of started to withdrawal then and kept to myself, but for the next two year. You wouldn't think anything was wrong. We moved to Maryland and stayed there for a little over a year and a half, till we came out to California. Stopping off in Southern California first and then going directly to Pacific Grove area and settled into a nice one bedroom apartment. This is where I got the courage to write to my aunt and put the return address on it. In the time that we left the farm to the present moment, I was afraid, scared, and all the rest of those emotions.

In time, I received a letter back from Jessica. I was so happy to hear from her. I didn't have the slights clue what she had in her letter. I read the letter several times, because I couldn't believe what I was reading. That a few short months after I left the area. My grandfather that I loved and honored and had so much respect for, died from lung cancer.

You can well imagine what was going through my mind. I blamed myself to the fullest. I thought he had died because I went away and would never come back or just broke his heart in some other fashion. I was mad as the Mad Hatter. I released some of the anger by telling God to let him come back and that I needed him so badly. By this time, those possibilities were out of the question. Though his spirit or energy may have been there without me knowing it and has been with me ever since.

This is where it really started, by putting this wall around myself and only allowing God, Jesus, The Holy

Spirit and my grandfather and mother into this circle. This is where the food becomes my friend and a companion. To soften the hurt, the pain and the torment. To get me through this, I watched a lot of movies, whether they were in the theater or on television. I guess my mind wanted to be distracted for those two to three hours, as the movies continued to play. From "Hamlet", to "The Ten Commandments" "Spartacus" to other great movies of that time and even ones before then. I must of seen at least a million or more movies in my whole life time.

Through Junior and Senior High School were the toughest. As everyone knows, kids can be curl. By them saying porky, chubby, there goes the fat pig. To other remarks. It really hurt, until I got to a level where, I didn't have the problem, because I always could lose the weight when I wanted too. The bullies or wise crackers would still have their problems. What really hurt was hearing it from adults. Or there goes Miss Piggy! Or tell you, you won't find any one, because you looking like an elephant and the fact most men would want someone like Kate Jackson.

I felt so alone. That's way I am so picky on who my friends are and believe me, there are not that many. Maybe that's why I like to write and have been interested in it for the longest time. So they could get to know me. I'm not great with the spoken work or they just don't want to understand, because we (as Americans) are so brain washed that we have to have that perfect size woman. Well, I can do the same thing to you men that are over weight also, but I wouldn't stoop that low. Even for the Cathy's of the world, we can lose the weight. You'll just find something else about us and you wouldn't still like us.

So the next time you see someone who is not that Chocolate pie. Who could be just ten pounds over weight to someone that maybe two hundred pounds over weight. Think of their feeling s before you might hurt their feelings.

I have to many scars inside me to tell you. But for a person like you, it would take to many years to teach how to be nice. I'm just glad that I'm not that size seven or a size zero.

Now that September 11th has happened, couldn't we change for the better by not calling other people names or to put labels on whoever it is. I know that I've put names on people, have you lately? We all had to change after that day. Would you want to make that a goal and change your mannerism. Would you give it a try, its not going to hurt you. It would be something good for a change. Things may turn in your favor, so you could get that fancy car.

Weight might be the number one subject here in America and discriminate against those who are in one way or another. For the Cathy's of this world, we have to stand up and fight. You may feel comfortable at whatever weight you are. We have to be United also.

We all have our problems. There is usually a reason beyond the scenes, just like in anything else and if we do not fix it, it won't be whole.

CHAPTER TEN

Take The Opportunity

What if you had an opportunity of a life time, to do something that you thought you would never come to you at all? Would you take it or will you let it slip through your fingers? Don't let your fears get in your way, because you feel secure in where your at. It could be that you don't want to do this something, because of some other fear. There is a time that you have to get onto that horse and just do it. This could be the chance that you were looking for. You may never know what may come of this. You may get other opportunities out of it besides. So, what are you waiting for? Did you ever think that maybe the Holy Spirit would want you to have this golden opportunity. It could be in your stars. Don't let John or Jane Doe hold you up or let your fear interfere with what could be your stepping stone to maybe your fortune. Especially, if certain things were to happen that could change your mind and it would hardly cost you any thing. A person is on this earth for a reason and the reason is he or she is meant to do X, Y and Z or if you prefer A, B and C. So what are you waiting for? Are you waiting until your sixty-five? You don't have to wait that long.

As the story goes. It went something like this. Over looking the great city of Philadelphia with all its glamour and sparkles and Independence that it has. A Continental Airlines flight was on its final approach to this fine airport. On this flight was a woman that had the GOLDEN OPPORTUNITY of a life time for four people to take. With a plan in mind. She would do it very wisely and knew how she wanted to do it. Even having the tickets with her. They certainly will be surprised. Not saying a thing until it was the right time.

A few hours later. I (Cathy) couldn't wait any longer. I am that woman on that Continental flight into this fine city of Philadelphia. I went into plan A. Of where I would just disquiet the possibilities with them. I wanted some feedback on what they would think about an opportunity like what I was going to give them. Imagine yourself in these peoples shoes.

We all were sitting in the living room of my cousin Patrick's home. It was like any other setting when a family gets together for a reunion or to spend time together. Plus meeting some people that I haven't met yet or haven't seen since they were in diapers a hundred years ago.

Rose (my aunt) looked over at me and wondered if there was something wrong. "Cathy, what's the matter, is there something wrong?" she said to me. (She was really concerned about the expression upon my face.)

"There is nothing wrong my good woman! I had just seen a vision. It said to me to ask the big question. Whatever that means. I told her.

"Well is there a question that you would like to ask me or someone in this room? Is it on the personal level or could everyone hear the question?" Rose had responded.

"I guess it would be the second part of your question, to where everyone could hear the question, because I would like some feedback on what is on my mind. The primary question is, What would four people think if they could go back to Los Angeles with me next Monday and spend eight to ten weeks out there. (Depending on their schedule.) Do all kinds of things, besides go to the Crystal Cathedral for those ten Sundays and during the time that they are there, they will have an opportunity to decide on their own, whether they would like to move out there and stay or to come home and continue your life here in New Jersey? There will be benefits to all this. You may never know what will happen next and wouldn't want to miss out on anything would you?" I said so proudly.

"What kind of price do we have to pay for getting something like this?" said Donald.

"Why do you think that there would be a price to pay? The person or persons in question may have paid the price, already. They could have earned it in some other way. Donald, you better do some thinking of your own. This could be a present from Jesus, for all you know or it could be the fact that I may think that its high time that some people get something out of life, instead of always serving others. There is one person in this room that has enough credits that would last them too many life times. So what do you have to say to that"? I said.

"Nothing!" he said. (He didn't know what the hay to say to that.)

"Good. Now we could get onto the next level. Are there any other questions? I said.

"Yes, I have one. What will happen, once those four people are out there?" said Max.

"My good man. There are some things that are meant to be a surprise. Even I don't have all the answers, but I will tell you this much. Whoever they are Max will have a barrel of fun. After that first week of adjust to Pacific time and all that." I said.

"Why a week?" said Max.

"With some of us, it does take a lot longer than others. Here, I'll give you a picture of what would happen if this would occur. The four people in question and myself would get up at three o'clock in the morning. (By this time the suitcases are already in the car that would be used to take us to the airport. Then all we have to do is to get ready and go. On the way to the airport, we would have to find a restaurant, somewhere and have something to eat. Even if its toast and jelly, because I do not who what they would be serving on the two flights we have to take to get there. I really would have to my homework to get a direct flight from Philadelphia to Los Angeles, if this thing was going to happen. Once out there, we would go to the apartment. Spend the afternoon with my mother and that evening we would go to "Medieval Times" and afterwards pickup some milk and some other things. Come home and retire early, because our bodies would still e on Eastern Standard Time. Then we could early start the next day. Lets say that a person would need some helpers to pack a two bedroom apartment and within a day or a day and a half could pack whatever. It would take team work and your cooperation. Then the movers would come and do their thing. Once in the new home, we could take out time to unpack whatever. Or just unpack it and get it over with. If we did that, then who knows what will happen then. From that point on would be the surprise." I said.

(They really got into it. Listening to every word that I said.) It looked like they were in some kind of shock or wanting something for a climax of some kind or watching a movie that maybe Stephen King wrote. It was something to see. There was no acting here! Things were coming back to normal with this group in slow motion.

Dana came out of it first. "If this was true, then you would need a vehicle like ours to get to the airport. Somewhere, we would have to trade cars somehow." She told us.

At this time, Dana, we are only talking about this, but thanks you for offering. Like I said before, I wanted to get some feedback and to see what you people would say to a question like this." I said.

"Cathy, what does it take to be one of those people, may I ask?" said Patty.

"Not much, I say, because if this was true. I would see it in that person's face, that was the chosen one. They would have a certain glow about them. So that I would know which one of you, Jesus would want me to take with me. (The four of them were there and their faces were glowing like nobody's business. It was a very special kind of glow. Sure, everyone was glowing from ear to ear, but it had to be the kind of glow that would come from Jesus. The ones that I did pick did have that certain glow.) They didn't know what to say or what to do. I figured that they were afraid of asking the wrong questions or say something that wouldn't make it so. Maybe that's why they were so silent. They all wanted to make sure that the four of them went and to make it happen. Of course, they didn't know which one of them would be the chosen one. There is a possibility that all of them wanted to be that person.

Rose knew what I meant when I started in again with describing what was going to happen in the eight to ten weeks while they were deciding whether they wanted to move or not. In that twenty minutes, I could see the glow around her get much brighter. I thought that if I had said that I was just trying it out on them that my aunt would be so disappointed, plus not forgetting the other three. Some of them would have to be, but not for Rose, Max, Thomas and Stacey. Out of twenty people it was hard to just pick those four. Sixteen of them would have those sad little faces, but I think they knew that I couldn't handle them all at once. I could have, but if I was told by God to only take those people, then the others would have to wait. Plus there is always one in the bunch that has to be the sour grapes.

"Hey, don't you think that you would want me to come and help with the moving and help you with the others on the airplane?" said Donald.

"Hey, don't you think that the job that you would have here would be as important then coming with us if you weren't on the list. Besides, if everyone cooperates with me, they will get on whatever plane and what makes you an expert on flying when you may not even taken a flight before. When I have more experience than anyone in this family. Just for that Donald, I do have an announcement to make and that four people will becoming with me to Los Angeles. I was going to do it a different way, but since Donald has to be the black sheep in the family and always has to put a damper on everything. I may as well come out with it. Oh yes, certain things will have to be done. Everything will fall into place, once the four people know who they are. Please, when your name is called, please don't run to your room or want to go back to your house and start packing. There will be plenty of time for that. If there are any questions, please don't be afraid to ask. Let me see, who is on this list. (I thought for a moment. So that they could stew.) Oh yea, now I know the names. Rose, Thomas, Stacey and let me see. Who would be number four? Would it be, no not that person. (Max was sweating there for a few minutes.) Well your wish will come true for Max. You are the fourth person." I said.

"Yippee, I can't believe it. I've won. When did you say you were going back to Los Angeles?" he asked.

From that point on, it was on the word go. Max made up his mind that he was going to move to California, even before see what the state was like or anything. I was right when I told my aunt sometime back that he would be coming to California, but I only thought it would be for a visits. God had other plans in mind for him. That he would become that great architect. A well known person of his time. Thomas and the others weren't sure about it. What we didn't know was that Max decided already. He did as he was told to do and acted like the others surprised, but he packed some extra things that he could into the suitcase that he had. Even into a duffel bag that belonged to him. I guess he figured that it would be less he would have to bring out on the second trip or if his grandmother would have to be concerned about it if she make that move to Los Angeles.

The ten weeks were like ten minutes. With the big move for some of them to be on a airplane from the very first time to helping me move from the apartment I was living in to a fine house. To getting the three of them into college of some kind. To helping my aunt get her stuff packed and onto a moving truck and get it started on its journey to California. While we flew over the country. Everyone had come out of this with something. They also become know for whatever kind of work they were in or were going to be in. Everyone was so happy.

Chapter Eleven
A Cold Chill One Night!

What would you say to this, if someone told you this story. Would you think that person was a little of their rocker, or had gone mad, or something? If the story was too unbelievable to your ears. Maybe, it could be the person's imagination, or they could have made the whole story up, you maybe thinking. Then, why would they dream up something so fantastic. Yes, there is the possibility that they wanted to drawn attention to themselves or they may want to be the center of attention, because they are not getting it from anywhere else. It may not be the person telling the story, it could by yourself, because you may have known this person all their life, and you may think of them in respect, when the case might be a totally different story. They could surprise you, one day. This could relate to anything that you may think about John or Jane Doe. This story maybe the story that will change your mind about them.

Here it is mid April of nineteen ninety-seven. It is like any other April day, though we here in Orange County California were having a cold spell. It was only in the upper fifties or sixties and in the night would be a lot colder. When a person is use to having it seventy-five to eighty degrees. It's quite a difference.

Here you are going about your own business. Trying to keep yourself warm. Then, night comes. You get yourself ready for bed with pleasant thoughts of all kinds of things and never expecting something like this would happen to you. You pull down your comforter and sheet. Then, of course, you sit onto the bed and of course you get yourself into a comfortable position. Whether you sleep alone, or with your husband or wife or maybe a small child. You fall asleep. Never expecting anything like this would happen to you. At two twenty in the morning you may have heard this voice, waking you up at this hour, (from a sound sleep.) You may have thought they were calling you for some reason or another. It could have been in your dream or vision, that you were having. This something had frightened you and you needed to get away from the danger. So, you wake up and get out of the bed. You look at the bed and around the room, but whatever had startled you wasn't there. You may think nothing of it. Then you discover that the room was so cold that you thought you were in a freezer or outside with just what you have on, and it's thirty-eight to forty degrees out there. Just remember what a piece of ice feels like. Well, that's the way that your body should feel like and the fact the room is at the same temperature.

You may of thought as long as you were up, you better slip into the bathroom. Once, you were finished, you had opened the door and quickly went back into your bed. So that you could warm yourself up once again. As you were getting into that comfortable position. You feel this warmth, like a double like in the middle of the road, but instead it is in the middle of your bed. You get yourself into the fetal position and throwing the sheet and the comforter over your head. Just treating this like any other time that you may have gotten up in the middle of the night. Slightly after, you had closed your eyes, (which could have been moments later. Which could have been right then or two minutes later.) The spirits do not have a time clock anymore. Then you start hearing this voice again, but this time, you didn't do anything about it. Because you may have been at peace with this, at this time. This voice was telling you all kinds of things that you did know about. And the voice of this person was from the other side. That could have been the cause of your awaking in the first place. You may not be use to receiving something like that, before. Or you weren't open to the fact, that things like this do really happen. (Of course, you may believe in God, and in Jesus or in the Holy Spirit and that there is a Heaven and a Hell.) But, there were some question marks in your mind.

Most people, don't believe in the dead coming back from the dead, to tell you a message of some kind who may just stand there and do nothing. That may guide you into something. It may save your life or find something that you thought you had lost, to finding that Gold Mine. Until you open up to the fact that it does happen, and that one day you may experience something so incredible or you may not, but, please be open to people, that do have these experiences. They may not be on the level of Spirituality as you are. You might have a high I.Q. but this person might have guidance or a message from whomever for you and you would be the only one that was called that special name by this person. Some people rather have E.Q. than I.Q. Life is to valuable to be doing something like that. Sadness is something you could get over, no matter how bad you feel.

This is what happen to me. I (Cathy) went through an experience like that. I never would have expected something like that to happen. Since, I wasn't close with the person in question. Even though we do have this certain fighting spirits and the fact that we were first cousins and live life the way we do. To bad that she had to die at a very young. She was only thirty-six or was it thirty-five years young. Oh well, God need her too.

I, like most people, couldn't believe what had happened. From being lifted out of the bed they way that I did and room feeling so cold like it was the dead of winter back in New York. I know better. I wasn't frighten by this, but I was more puzzled by it, than anything else. I had to have some wild dream of some kind. That had frighten me so badly that made me respond the way that I did. It must have be something, it had too be, to make me move the way that I did. Especially, if a person weighs two hundred and fifty pounds.

After clearing my head and fallen asleep. The time was going quickly to the time in question. At two thirty that morning. I must have seen her just standing there. I didn't know that it was her, because she may have head her hair differently, after Jesus helped her get back to being herself. When she did speck, that's when I must of jumped out of the bed and though that I was being lifted out. I didn't think she would come to me. I just didn't believe it. This was big time for me. I first looked at the bed and then around the room, to see if she was there, but nothing. Then I realized that the room was so cold that I thought I was standing outside in my night shirt. It was like ice. I figured that as long as I was up. I would take a little walk to the bathroom, before any of it had froze. The windows were closed, there was no fan on or any other machine was on to blow the cool air around. So any of that would be out of the question. So what could we say.

I was figuring that I was dreaming all this and that's all it could be. I went back to sleep. I wanted to be warm and comfortable and hopefully dream of something else that I could cope with. I went right to sleep. I didn't go past go and collect two hundred dollars.

The Holy Spirit wanted to finish his job, so that the chain could be continues and to tell the people. So that the people could be content and continue to pray to the Lord God and to Jesus Christ.

I guess this had to be a special night for me. I figured out later that the reason why the Holy Spirit was using me, was because in a sense, I had used my cousin Judy several years ago, without knowing it or what would have happened to her in nineteen ninety. I wished that it didn't happen to her, or for anyone else, to go through what she did. Of being hit by a truck. Then dying twice and being sent back to earth, because it wasn't her time to go. With her jaw all messed up and her nose out of joint. To go through the pain that was out of this world and having operation after operation up to a point. Apparently the doctor told her about the last and final operation and told her whatever information she needed to know. The one part had scared her and she didn't want to go through anymore pain. Especially if was going to be a lot worse than it already has and this would last for at least a year and a half. Judy didn't want that. Would you blame here? She went on with this for sometime, till finally she agreed to go through with it.

God put his two cents into it. I (Cathy) do not know the main reason why God had to take a young woman of thirty five or thirty six years old, but that is too young. To have her take too much of her medication to slow her heart down and went with the angel of death to the pearly gates of Heaven or to where the light begins. Helped by the guardian angel and maybe someone that they loves so dearly.

Though, when I called Judy's mother and told her all this. She told me that she was just outside with the dog and was praying to Jesus to see if Just was all right and made it to His great Kingdom. Rose (Judy's mother) was so pleased to hear that. Of course, she wanted to know more, but there wasn't anymore.

Though now, I think that God wants Rose to go onto a great adventure. Now that a period of time has gone by. So, if there's anytime that you may get an opportunity to do something then do it. I am talking about something beyond just the ordinary opportunities. You will have to over come whatever fears you may have if someone said to you, "How would you like to live in California and that all your moving expenses would be paid for. Never knowing what's around the next corner. Plus live in this great house and who knows what would happen after that. It's an offer that can be refused, but a person would miss out on a lot of things and the fact that they could start their own business out here and could become well know by their talents whatever they maybe.

You can over come your fears or whatever is holding you back from taking that opportunity, that may come in your way. This goes for everyone, not just for Rose, but anyone that is reading this story. I know that it is easy to use an excuses to let some great adventure or opportunity go by. Then sometime down the road, you kick yourself in the shines for not doing it. Or as your sitting there and wondered what would have happened if I did take that offer. Whether it was a career move, or just to be in a better location for whatever reasons you may have. You may tell whomever it was, that the answer would have to be no. You are telling God the very same thing. Wake up people. It's not about God, it's about you. Things maybe secure on the level that your on, but let's give something else a chance and just adventure onto something you maybe wanted to do for years or for a very short time.

If I could stand the cold for the one night. A kind of cold that comes with the person that comes to visit with you, when they are from the other side. Though I didn't see anyone at all. It was my cousin Judy at this time. I guess it wasn't meant to be, to see her in that form or that she didn't want to scare me. She would of surprised me that's all.

So if I could do this for one night, you can reach for that impossible star of making that impossible dream come true.

CHAPTER TWELVE
THE SUNSET

What do you think of when you see a sunset? Do you daydream? Does it make you think of something special or you may think of something that happened in the past or will it be their future? What will this sunset bring you?

As I tell my story to the writer of this piece. When I saw this photo of this sunset. The water was so still that it could be used as a stage and could see the other side of the pond and the gray clouds were the background. I could see myself with my cousin Maxwell landing at the Portland Airport. Neither one of us knew what we were going to get ourselves into. Though I (Cathy) had the upper hand on this, because I knew what this place was like and what he was in for. The place is called "Bearnstow" in the town of Mt. Vernon. A place where you could learn about the great outdoors and a lot of other things.

As we went up to 295 to the 95 to get to Augusta. So we could stay in town for a few days, to have a few days there and get some supplies and to giving Maxwell a great tour. These two months would stay with him for the rest of his life. For a man that is twenty-one years old and higher than a kite, because it is in his spirit, to have adventure.

As we turned into the driveway, in which it was a long one, but not even a mile. Maxwell went into more of amazement. His thoughts were that we were going into his own little world. In many ways, it is for each individual. He was making his own memories, starting from the word, paradise. I, on the other hand have been down this driveway so many times, that I have lost count. Coming here for over forty years, you think that it is your home away from home. It is a paradise for me too.

Maxwell got what he wanted. To run it for the summer. At Bearnstow, he would get this feeling, even though there were modern convinces and a cabin to sleep in, but everything else deals with the outdoors, (most everything.) From riding a horse, to swimming, to sawing wood, to using an ax, to pitching a tent, to knocks, to everything else that the place provides. At first he thought that he was in boot camp, instead of a camp where you learn these different things. I must have been some kind of General. Every morning. I got him up at seven a.m. It takes him sometime to wake up and do his morning routine. He couldn't have breakfast in bed. It is not allowed. I wasn't going to start by bringing him a cup of coffee, so he could drink it on the porch of number eight. Each building has a number in the living quarters and other buildings are named. Once he got use to the idea and get into the routine. Maxwell was ready to face each day with a happy smile upon his face. The days got easier, as the time went on.

I thought at first that it wasn't going to be easy, because I thought he might have his expectation on very high. That it was some kind of resort, and it is, but not in the way he thought it might be. A young man that wanted a lot of input and received it too. Writing everything down, so he wouldn't forget. Plus all the photographs that were taken by him. It will cost him a fortune. The joy in his face was so bright, a person would need a pair of sun glasses. I was glad for that. Plus for Maxwell to learn all that he did. With all the classes and to learn the lingo that goes around there. We both learned a lot. It wasn't just Maxwell, but I did the same, since I am the one that sponsored him in the first place. Maybe it was my expectations that were to high or thought in the wrong direction as usual.

When the time was getting short. I asked Maxwell to start thinking of packing his things. Of what he wasn't going to be using from then until we got back to California.

He didn't want to leave. He wanted to stay longer, but that it wasn't possible because of other obligations and I did not feel like taking another class. Two classes were enough for me. I thought that after taking the two, I would be so relaxed that I didn't want to be jumping around or whatever the teacher would have us do. I had all ready talked with her and she told me that she was going to have a lot of jumping exercises and motions. Some piece she learned in Africa when she went a few months ago.

Little by little, we both started to pack. Though we did have two weeks and could of done it a couple of days before, but I didn't feel like doing things at the last minute. I even packed a care box to sent home so we would have to bother with it. Once we got the suitcases packed. I asked Maxwell to put them into the trunk of the rent-a-car and we could use the duffel bags for whatever was left.

It's hard for me to leave. Though each time it is easier as time goes on, because we both know that we could come back at anytime. I checked the cabin one more time, since I was up there for another reason. We both walked to the clearing where the car was parked. Saying so long for now and to deliver a message to my mother from Ruth the woman that has this place.

Thanks to "Bearnstow" for the time there and for the people that helped Maxwell get his education in the woods. As we flew up and away.

This is what I saw in my sunset. The place is real and this is what I saw when I took the photograph. What do you see in it?

This chapter is a piece I would like to do for Maxwell. Though he may not know it, yet, but soon he will. Though I may change it a little. That we would travel by car cross country so we could see America together and to have the car on the other end.

A Tribute

IN MEMORY OF EVELYN ACKLEY
Born October 25, 1959
TO
Dead November 6, 1996

This is for someone that has only lived for thirty-six years. Has helped in so many ways, even after her death in November of Nineteen ninety-six.

Sometimes, you ask yourself, Why does God take the young?" "Why does He do these things to us for?" Sure, there are lessons to be learned or we have to pay the price, but what gives?

Yes, you're going to tell me, that God has other plans for the dear woman. The question is, what? No one will have that answer. Maybe, the answer would be the little messenger girl. To be that little helper of some kind, to draw the bridge a lot closer from Heaven to the earth, at least for some of us here on this world of ours.

Is Evelyn Ackley going to be the one that will be the one that will move the mountain for us, once we get onto the right track or will she encourage us to go forward with what is meant for us to be doing, no matter what it is. Is this going to be our ace in the hole? Good questions! Now for the questions needed to be answered, in God's time, maybe not in this story.

I wasn't very close with her, but she was come to me. I did love her, as a cousin should love their cousins. I guess I'm still a little stunned about her death. But I'm glad that she doesn't have to go through anymore pain or have the final operation that she needed to have.

The future will tell. No one knows what is going to happen in the next few seconds or the next few minutes or days, but I think that there will be a lot of communication from her, because she is the type that just doesn't sit there and does nothing or lets anything slip by her. Evelyn is the kind of person that just doesn't sit there and does nothing or lets anything slip by her. Evelyn is the kind of person that like to talk and gets everything said. No matter how much time the Lord Jesus will let her, now that she is with Him. Evelyn can really be a conversationalist and could tell you where she stands and to put you in your place, if need be.

Though Evelyn wasn't a public figure of any kind, but she was well-known in her own right. She touched so many people in her short life, even if you weren't that close to her as a friend or family member. She maybe tough on the outside, but she also could be a sweet as a chocolate, if she wanted to.

Be at peace, my good woman. Things will be all right, here on earth. Just talk with Jesus and ask Him if it would be all right, if that dram that I've been having would come true. The one I'll call "The Giver That Got Her Gift, After All These Years". So I could help your mother, brothers and sister and the rest of the family, plus the Crystal Cathedral. So that other things could be done also for other people that may need the help. I am not thinking of myself, but for others, I know that you'll come and visit every so often to give me messages for whomever. So do you think that you could do that for little ole me. The story is written, but it doesn't not belong with these short works, because it hasn't happened as yet.

Chapter Thirteen

"THAT'S IT FOLKS!!"

There is no more surprises and nothing else to tell. The only thing I could say is that all this happened in a ten year period. God had me working all right, with all these chapters. There isn't a final curtain here, because there is more to come.

I hoped you enjoyed what you have read and that it could help you in a situation like in a few of the chapters.
A TRIBUTE TO A MAN I LOVED, BUT LOST SO YOUNG.

Here is a man who could harm anyone, if he wanted too. He was a very easy going kind of person. Someone you wouldn't want them to miss the party or at your place of business or have work for you. He was the kind of man that you would want around.

This is the way I feel about him. We were so compatible with each other and I always wanted to be with my Grandfather for some reason or another. Harry Duby, was my hero, a man I would love so much that it was way off the charts. He would be the kind of person I wouldn't want to marry, if I could. We all know we can not get what we want in this world of ours, unless by a miracle that we find this kind gentleness and caring and loving personality. The warmth fro him could be seen for miles.

In Nineteen Sixty Two, when I heard of his death. I went into a shock that has lasted for so many years, because he died a little more than two years prior. Since no knew where I was, I couldn't be there. I know I never did get the closure I needed with his death. Going through a kind of hell with this. I couldn't believe that he left me and believing I killed him with a heartache or gave him the disease that he really died from. Since then I have clocked my first twelve years of life. As everyone can figure out is,

119

because of the pain and the memory of my Grandfather. With all the times we did spend together. I felt special, like I was a princess. Though I was his little Shadow, like in the song "ME AND MY SHADOW". My heart will always have him in there and I will never forget him. I have gone to another level and gone beyond. Now I am moving on. I have put him on a high mountain, because in a sense he was the only man that I truly love and returned the love and support I needed. A very special person for me. There are no words that can explain it. He will always be at my side, until the day we meet in Heaven.

You're the one that is special, GRANDPA
THIS ONE IS FOR YOU
I LOVE YOU, STILL

ABOUT THE AUTHOR

Since I was a young child I always loved to write and to tell stories, and I always had everyone listening to every word. I love to travel and experience new things, so there could be more stories. Plus, I love to take photos to help explain what may be happening at one point in time. I love to do a lot of things like any other person.

But people just stay away, because I guess they don't like to be friends with a person who has a weight problem. I am never alone, and I'm not afraid of anything.